ann Educational Books, Inc.
over Street   Portsmouth, NH 03801-3959
and agents throughout the world

ld like to thank the teachers, children, and parents who have
eir permission to include material in this book. Every effort has
ade to contact copyright holders for permission to reprint bor-
material where necessary, but if any oversights have occurred,
ld be happy to rectify them in future printings of this work.

ledgments for previously published material are on page xi.

of Congress Cataloging-in-Publication Data

romise : redefining reading and writing for "special"
ents / edited by Susan Stires.
    p.   cm.
cludes bibliographical references.
BN 0-435-08573-5
    Learning disabled children—Education—Language arts.
anguage arts—Remedial teaching.   3. Language experience
roach in education.   4. Special education—Language arts.
tires, Susan.
704.85.W58   1991
9'0446—dc20   91-6550
                                          CIP

n by Maria Szmauz
d in the United States of America
2 93 94 95   10 9 8 7 6 5 4 3 2 1

With Promis

Redefining Reading and Writ
for "Special" Stude

Edited

Susan Stir

The Center for Teaching and Lea
Edgecomb, N

Heinem
Portsmouth, New Hamp

For Julia and Anne, who made me
a real teacher, and for Kinne, who
loves to learn

. . . if you set up the right conditions, try as best you can to cross class and cultural boundaries, figure out what's needed to encourage performance, . . . if you watch and listen, again and again there will emerge evidence of ability that escapes those who dwell on differences.

from *Lives on the Boundary*
by Mike Rose

Contents

I. Real Reading and Real Writing

II. Portraits of Readers and Writers

Acknowledgments

Philippa Stratton and Nancie Atwell have supported me from the time I had the idea for this book, and I thank them for it. Philippa has been encouraging and patient all along the way. Nancie, who is my teacher, colleague, and friend, convinced me that I have something to say and the means by which to say it. For that, I am most grateful. I am also grateful to Alan Huisman, who has expertly guided the book through production.

"Third Strike," by Tom Romano, was previously published in the April 1987 issue of *Language Arts,* copyright 1987 by the National Council of Teachers of English, and is reprinted with permission.

"Growing as a Writer: L.D. and All," by Susan Stires, and "Remembering Bernice," by Patricia Tefft Cousins, were previously published in *Insights,* vol. 22, no. 6 (Spring 1990), and are reprinted with permission.

"The Student with Learning Disabilities in a Writing-Process Classroom," by William L. Wansart, was previously published in the *Journal of Reading, Writing and Learning Disabilities,* vol. 4, no. 4 (1988/89), and is reprinted with permission of Hemisphere Publishing Corporation.

"All Children Can Write," by Donald H. Graves, was previously published in the Fall 1985 issue of *Learning Disabilities Focus* and is reprinted with permission.

"Revaluing Readers and Reading," by Kenneth S. Goodman, was previously published in the January 1982 issue of *Topics in Learning & Learning Disabilities,* copyright 1982 by the Aspen Systems Corporation, and is reprinted with permission.

Figure 16–1, on page 160, was used previously in an article by Janis I. Bailey entitled "Problem Solving Our Way to Alternative Evaluation Procedures," published in the April 1988 issue of *Language Arts,* copyright 1988 by the National Council of Teachers of English. Reprinted with permission.

Introduction

With Promise started out to be a book about teaching reading and writing to special education students. It was this population that I first learned from when I applied the principles of process to writing and reading. Working with those who were labeled learning disabled, emotionally disturbed, and educable mentally retarded, I saw readers and writers. I saw learners striving for meaning in their lives and in the world, striving through language. And I looked closely. For the past ten years, in both the resource room and the regular classroom, I conducted research to learn how my students learn and how I can best learn from them in order to teach.

There are many other teachers and researchers, in both special education and general education, who share my concerns about providing the most sensible instruction possible for their "special" students. They see needs as possibilities. They recognize that the development, experiences, and processes of some readers and writers resemble long winding paths more than smooth superhighways. They strive to know who each student is, not only as a reader and writer, but also as a person. And they respond to what their students are trying to do. Some of them have joined me in putting this book together to address teachers' concerns about "special" students in process classrooms. Others have already contributed to the growing body of knowledge of teaching reading and writing to students considered to be in need. Of the existing literature, there are only a few books devoted to this topic. Additionally, there are chapters scattered throughout books on literacy education. They include Nancie Atwell's chapter and my chapter in *Understanding Writing* (Heinemann 1988). There are also Carol Avery's case study in *Seeing for Ourselves* (Heinemann 1987) and mine on evaluation in *Stories to Grow On* (Heinemann 1989).

In the process of developing into a book, *With Promise* has become more than it started out to be. It has turned out to be a book about teaching reading and writing to any elementary students considered to be outside the mainstream, not just special education students. Just as the lines are becoming blurred between special education, remedial reading, and other groups deemed to be "at risk," the lines here are blurred. And so they should be. Most of the categories were originally created to better understand needs and provide services according to those needs. The intention was good, perhaps even noble, but the effect has probably been more damaging than beneficial. All of the categories define students in terms of their limitations. Even ESL has a deficiency connotation in this country, although it should have a different implication. I believe that the effect is to further limit students and to create almost unscalable social barriers.

Someday we may look back on what we have done in creating special groups and special instruction and see it as comparable to what teachers did fifty years ago when they forced left-handed children to write with their right hand. Education has been molding rather than liberating. Our tendency is to squeeze instruction through our logic rather than to try to see the logic through which children act, and then follow and support it. Glenda Bissex, in *GNYS AT WORK: A Child Learns to Write and Read,* says, " . . . the logic by which we teach is not always the logic by which children learn" (Cambridge, MA: Harvard University Press, 1980, 199). Her reference is to **all** children, including special education, remedial, ESL, and other designated groups of children. The writers of the chapters of *With Promise* follow in order to lead; they understand the value of process and product; and they are concerned with the whole student, not one split into strengths and weaknesses.

The first section describes programs of real reading and real writing. It begins with Alfreda Furnas's story of her efforts to change the school experiences of her elementary resource room kids. Throughout her chapter, Alfreda provides descriptions of individual students and moments in her classroom. She found that her greatest challenge in teaching her students was one of the heart, not of the head. Next, Marie Dionisio writes about her work with sixth-grade remedial readers and takes us on a journey through the school year. The students arrive, hating reading and writing and expecting the skill exercises that they had in the past, and they leave reading the same books as their nonremedial peers and making book lists for the summer.

Esther Sokolov Fine, a primary teacher and former learning disabilities teacher, shows how nine of her special education students collaborated to produce an oral text and how they broke through their barriers of silence. Some special students speak very little in elementary school because their schooling experiences contrast sharply with their life experiences. No wonder learning is often difficult for them. Ilene Seeman Johnson, a middle school special education teacher, writes about reading aloud—the heart of her reading program. Like Furnas, she takes a strong stand as she tells this story of collaboration with students at risk academically and affectively.

Mainstreaming all special students is a reality in some schools. Michael Quinn, a learning disabilities specialist in such a school, relates how he teaches specific reading and writing skills to his students. Michael provides a series of vignettes that allows the reader to see and hear the teaching/learning interactions with a variety of identified, mainstreamed students. Karen Robinson—who wears two hats in a small rural school, principal and Chapter 1 teacher— examines the problems of pull-out programs and describes how she schedules herself into primary classrooms. Karen considers her program a model if the classroom is a literate environment.

Much of the talk in special education and other groups concerned with students "in need" is about where to deliver services. Pull-out programs have many disadvantages; keeping students in the classroom has a number of advantages. However, putting a specialist in the classroom or training the classroom teacher to take the role of the specialist is not necessarily the solution to the problems of pull-out programs. If the stance toward the learner remains one of "fixing" him or her, we will achieve nothing, except to create a pull-out program within the classroom. Although I have long been an advocate of "put-in," scheduling myself into classrooms long before it was "in fashion," I did so only if the classroom was a literate environment and the students were part of a community of learners. I applaud the efforts of the many schools, like Stratham Elementary School in Stratham, New Hampshire, that are working to create those environments in order that students can be mainstreamed and specialists can be support personnel. However, that means a lot of change for regular education. Rather than being an advocate of pull-out or put-in, for now I am an advocate of having kids in "a place where they are treated as fascinating individuals to whom we listen as well as speak, a place where they participate in every possible way" (Robert Hale, "Musings," *The Horn Book,* vol. 65, no. 5, 1989, 665). That may be a classroom, a resource room, or another environment.

The second section contains five chapters of case studies, which serve both as research and forms of evaluation. They are the stories of individual students for whom learning to read and write (or learning to read and write better) was achieved in programs of real reading and real writing. Case study research helps inform the field and develop theoretical knowledge. It is also one of the most practical approaches to instruction that teachers can take. In conducting a case study, we are getting inside a reader and writer's processes. We learn about that reader and writer, and our evaluation is constantly informing our teaching. We try to do this with all of our students; documentation yields us case studies.

The first chapter is my two-year study of an intermediate-level learning disabled student. It is also the story of the many things we taught each other as I learned to teach writing and the student learned to write. In the chapter that follows, Patricia Tefft Cousin provides a longitudinal study of a girl who was her student in an inner-city public school. The student's struggles with literacy became a catalyst for Pat to learn more about language and learning difficulties beyond what was offered in special education.

Teacher-researcher Joan Throne believes very strongly in providing authentic reading and writing experiences and in including special education, remedial, and ESL students in her classroom. Given these experiences, she believes that students learn from one another, and here she describes the growth of an ESL student. William Wansart is the researcher who worked with Michael Quinn in setting up the mainstream program at Quinn's school. In his case study, William describes what the student learned about writing and reading, as well as the classroom context in which this learning occurred. In the last chapter in this section, I provide two portraits of first-grade students identified as having language difficulties. Here, I identify classroom conditions, describe the idiosyncrasies of the students, and relate their most significant reading and writing experiences during their first formal year of schooling.

The five chapters in the third section are a rationale for teaching "special" students through reading and writing process and whole-language approaches. These chapters are also about change for students and ourselves. In his chapter, Donald Graves affirms that children with learning problems can and should write; they should not be disenfranchised from literacy. He provides a clear overview of writing process and the establishment of a classroom community. Kenneth Goodman extends the discussion to reading by proposing that "readers in trouble" be revalued and taught in the most sensible, realistic ways possible. He urges us to look at reading as an interactive, constructive process, and at readers as language users capable of using their language. Bonnie Sunstein explores the gaps between life's meaning and school's work, gaps that could be bridged if literacy research and special education practice were connected and implemented. She shows instances where it has been bridged and its effects, but calls for more.

Linda Hoyt, a special education curriculum specialist, envisions ways of knowing that transcend the verbal, but also enhance it. She proposes the integration of the expressive arts with literary activities for all students, and especially those with learning difficulties. She helps keep our thinking fresh and forward-looking. Janis Ivanowsky Bailey reflects on her development as a teacher. As a specialist who has returned to the classroom, she sees her role as an expanding, effective one and writes about it to show her progression.

The final section consists of two conversations. They are models for our own conversations about our "special" students and the teaching and learning opportunities and invitations that we provide them. Ellen Aragon, Patricia Tefft Cousin, Cathy Leonard, Linda Prentice, Lisa Ann Rose, and Timothy Weekley collaborated to write about how they applied holistic understandings about language and learning to their teaching of special-needs students. They point out that they are not offering a panacea but an invitation to join the discussion. The last chapter is also a discussion, one by Carmelita Chee, Clark Etsitty, Lee and Daisy Kiyaani, Louise Lockhard, and Laura Tsosie, who all work together in a school on a Navajo reservation. By looking thoughtfully at their community, these teachers are beginning to define literacy in meaningful terms for a cultural group traditionally considered outside the mainstream of education.

The featured writers are teachers and researchers who, in most cases, have made helping "special" students their life's work. Their insights and expertise provide evidence not only of their theoretical understandings but also of effective practices. I am grateful to all of the writers of these chapters, and I hope that their voices will be heard inside and outside literacy circles. I also hope that this book will encourage others who work hard with "special" students to write and share what they know and do.

Prologue. Third Strike

Tom Romano

The final two months of school we fifth graders played softball during every recess. And we played for keeps. Each team sought to score runs in double figures, all in one inning if possible. But Kenny, Steve, and Wayne hampered these high powered offensive plans. They couldn't hit. They were always sure outs, dribbling balls back to the pitcher, tipping fouls to the catcher. And worst of all, they usually struck out.

Such ineptitude at the plate didn't sit well with the hard-hitting boys of the fifth grade, those who belted line drives into gaps and deep flies over the outfielders' heads. These sluggers took steps to limit the inning-ending strikeouts of Kenny, Steve, and Wayne. They began "claiming third strikes." It worked this way. Charging in from the field after putting the other team out, the sluggers began making their claims.

"I get Kenny's third strike!" yelled one.

"I get Steve's!"

"I get Wayne's!"

And that settled it. When one of those weak-hitting boys came to the plate, he did not own his time at bat. Instead of three strikes, three errors, three freewheeling swings at the ball, he was allowed only one. For if he committed that second error—strike two—the slugger who had claimed his third strike took over. The weak-hitting boy stepped aside; the slugger strode to the plate and socked the next good pitch. The weak hitter then played out a fraudulent role, running the bases as though the hit were his.

The pressure to produce was great on Kenny, Steve, and Wayne. When they entered the batter's box, you could see anxiety in their desperate eyes, their fierce grip on the bat, their nervous foot movement. They could not relax. They could not concentrate on the pitch, because they knew they were not going to get all their cuts—three, if necessary, and another three the next time at bat, and another three after that. As they stood in the batter's box, awaiting the arching softball, they knew they mustn't make a mistake.

Two of the weak hitters began purposely swinging amiss in order to gain a kind of acceptance from the sluggers who had claimed their third strikes.

These sluggers, of course, grew ever more disdainful of those two obsequious boys. In the minutes before recess, or on the way to school, perhaps even in their dreams, Kenny, Steve, and Wayne must have anguished about their turns at bat. They knew that as they stood at the plate, struggling to hit the softball, more capable boys hovered nearby, hoping for their failure, eager to successfully finish their time at bat and extend a big inning.

The fifth-grade softball games continued right up to the edge of summer. The sluggers' batting averages swelled as they slammed blazing grounders, crisp line drives, towering home runs. And Kenny, Steve, and Wayne?

They never learned to hit.

I. Real Reading and Real Writing

When we
home. So
and we
back to
they

1. Yes, You Can!

Alfreda B. Furnas

"I know how to read and how to write" writes seven-year-old Melody. She slides her paper across the table for me to read. I smile and say, "Yes, you do!" She retrieves the paper and, tongue between teeth, writes another sentence: "I can read now." Again, she slides the paper across to where I am sitting. Again, I smile and say, "Yes, you can!" She takes her paper back, and with great care writes, sounding out words. When she gives it back to me, she has added five more sentences. This time she leans over my shoulder, pointing at each of her words with a pencil, and proudly reads to me:

I know how to read and how to write. I can read now. I can read to Miss Furnas. I can read to everybody. I can read to myself. I can read to my mom and dad. I can read to my aunt and uncle.

Although ten weeks ago Melody couldn't read and write, she can now and knows it. With a hug I tell this tiny second grader, "Oh yes, you can!"

I came to teach special-needs children from a regular elementary school background. I had spent my own school years suffering the slings and arrows of a child with school learning problems in the fifties, and have a child of my own with school learning problems. However, I started my tenure as a special education teacher with no formal training in teaching children with special needs. As a resource room teacher, I wondered if the reading and writing approach I'd used successfully in kindergarten (Furnas 1985) and in first and third grade would work with special-needs students.

I had expected my greatest challenge in teaching children with reading delays would be helping them to crack the code of print. I was wrong. I think all children want to read and write. If they can't read by the age of six, they get discouraged. Once they are behind in reading, they are placed in a low reading group, becoming both discouraged and isolated. In a second-grade class of thirty, they stand out. They know it. Though these children have different problems affecting their learning, they all have one thing in common: fear about themselves as readers, as writers, as learners. I found my greatest challenge in teaching these students was one of the heart, not of the head.

Edward walks through the halls carrying a sack full of papers. These aren't just any papers; they're his manuscripts. It doesn't matter to ten-year-old Ed that he writes on primary paper with 1½-inch line spaces. It doesn't matter that his spelling is less than standard. He can read it, and they're his stories. When I remark about the difficulty of toting around this four-inch stack, he replies, "I can't help it. I just write all the time. There's nothing to do at home, so I just write and write. I guess I'm just a writin' fool!"

I find it hard to recognize this Edward. One year ago he wouldn't write at all. He had great difficulty with his fine motor skills, his letter/sound associations were almost nonexistent, and his reading was at least one year below his grade level. He told me constantly how stupid he was. When truly exasperated with himself, he would not only tell me he was stupid, but that he was going to kill himself. Today he reads above grade level. He seldom tells me how stupid he is.

Clay cautiously approaches. "Is this how you spell turtles?"

I look at his word "turdues" and reply, "You spelled all the sounds you heard!" His face lights with accomplishment, and, all third-grade legs, he skips back to his desk to continue writing. Clay has only been in my resource room for three days. He has never been allowed to use inventive spelling before. He is anxious that his weak phonetic knowledge is inadequate to spell the words he wants to use. He does not yet believe that his spelling will not be evaluated, corrected, marked. As the week progresses, Clay asks less help of me, seeking out other children when he feels the need, or sounding words out on his own. He begs for extra time to write. He has long-awaited stories to tell.

There is no great teaching magic at work here, but there is kid magic: kid confidence and kid determination. As a teacher, my main task is simple. I must convince children, in their hearts, that they *can* learn, and give them the skills to do it. Failure paralyzes children. By the time children reach a special education classroom most of them feel like failures and will tell you so. They demonstrate it in their hostile or passive approach to academic tasks, or school in general. They feel small and unimportant, overwhelmed by what they *can't* do. Very often these kids come from classes and homes where teachers and parents have given up on them. They are not expected to achieve. They are babied, or worse, ignored. Most truly believe that they are stupid. They don't expect much from themselves. And so my first stop on the way to their hearts is to have high expectations of them and to enable them to experience success.

I expect them to learn to read. I expect that they will learn to write and do math. I tell them that I expect them to achieve. I tell them that they are smart. I expect them to behave well. Although I acknowledge that they have trouble learning the way most kids do, I tell them that they *can* learn. I tell them in class, in the hall, in the lunchroom, in the mall. Our school psychologist once remarked, "The thing with you is, you don't act like you're teaching children with learning problems. You run that resource room like the gifted program." "Thank you" were the only words that came to mind.

In addition to having high expectations for all the children, I set reasonable, achievable expectations for each child so that she can be successful. When I teach, I want to be teaching children who feel successful and empowered. I accept the child where he is, then ever so delicately stretch that child by setting an expectation that is just barely out of reach . . . just barely. Newkirk refers to this theoretically as Vygotsky's zone of proximal development, that area where a child needs only a slightly higher experience or model to move ahead (Newkirk 1989). This sort of stretching requires fine-tuning for each child. I involve the children in my thinking as I set my expectations for them. Soon they are setting their own.

On her second day in my class, Amanda anxiously tells me that her teacher says she needs to learn to spell her last name. I reply, "Do you know what it starts with?"

She answers, "W."

"Do you know the next letter?"

"H."

"Well, I'm not worried. I think you'll know the whole thing by the end of next week!" She smiles a rare smile and gets to work. The next day she knows the first four letters.

Jake comes to my side, book in hand. "I expect that you'll want me to go to a harder book, now that I can read this one." I think he is wise to me.

In order for children to take risks, to accept the challenge of going beyond their comfortable level, they must feel safe. I've tried to establish my classroom as a community of learners. Students know that they don't work alone. It is a place where we grow together and as individuals; a place where expectations are high, but where it is safe and normal to make mistakes. It is a place where small steps and hard work are valued, and where learners make decisions and take responsibility for their own learning.

We know that good readers and writers constantly make decisions as they interact with print (Hansen 1987). In order to make decisions, children need to have choices. Unfortunately, there are few choices left to children in the elementary school. From when they get a drink of water to what they have for lunch, there are no choices, no decisions. There are many choices that I cannot offer my students. I am mandated by law to teach required skills set for the child's instructional grade level. They can't decide when they come to my class, because I work out the schedule. They can't choose on which nights they will have homework; this is set by school policy.

However, there are many choices that I can offer my students, and I do. When my students work, they may decide where they sit and with whom they work. Since I do not assign topics for their writing, they choose their own topics. They may decide on paper style and writing implement. They determine if their work is to be shared or published. They choose the books they are going to read (Hansen 1987). A skeptical colleague asks me, "But don't they just read all the easy stuff over and over again?" I have to agree that this does happen once in a while, and the child needs a nudge to move on, but generally the children accept the expectation that once they have reached the point of mastery, they can and will move ahead. Success does that. Children want more of it, and so, when they know that success is possible, they willingly accept a challenge. I wonder why we so often ignore this powerful motivator.

I know that reading aloud to children is important, and I read to my students every day (Anderson 1984). Through reading aloud, I show my excitement about reading and my joy for books. It introduces children to books and authors and shows them a level of writing they may not yet be able to read. Through it I can expose my students to a variety of genres and writing styles. As I read aloud, I can demonstrate what goes on inside my head as I read. Mostly, reading aloud to children can help develop in them a love of stories. So many of my children have not been read to at home. Some of their parents are illiterate. My fifth graders begged me to read nursery rhymes from Mother Goose. On their own they discovered three different versions of *The House that Jack Built* in the school library, which they brought to the class to be read. John has enjoyed the rhyme so much that this morning he chose it to read to the first-grade class we read with every other week. At the age of ten, these half-grown kids are enjoying an experience with stories that they should have had when they were preschoolers.

As I read one of the *Three Investigators* mysteries to my fourth-grade group, I let the children see my thought processes as I read. I talk about what background knowledge I bring to the story that is helping me understand what I am reading. Aloud, I try to predict what may happen next. I stop and detail what I think may be a clue and why. Luckily, there are some forty of these well-written mysteries, so that as I read a book new to me, I can show the children genuine responses to what I am reading.

I don't always read stories that are new to me. I often read stories that are favorites of mine. Children pick up on the enthusiasm and excitement I experience in sharing a book I love. Tammy lets me know that I'm on the right track when she tells me, "Mrs. Furnas, you know how *The Mouse and the Motorcycle* is one of your favorite books? Well, *Little House on the Prairie* is one of mine!"

I do teach skills, including phonics, so that children learn letter/sound associations. The children see, hear, say, and write the letters and their corresponding sounds as part of their spelling program. I do not teach miles of phonics rules that apply only once in a while, but I do teach generalizations like the VCE pattern, which often helps in reading or writing an unknown word. Instead of using follow-up workbooks, my students do real writing. This writing provides the "whole" to the "part" of phonics. Children get to see that what they learn is immediately usable as they write using inventive spelling. I believe that writing is critical to learning to read. Time and time again, I see progress in writing precede progress in reading.

I wish all my students would turn into "writing fools," like Edward. What do we write? Personal narrative, stories, chapter books, imitations of current movies, poems, letters, signs, and notes. My second and third graders wrote a series of stories with an idea borrowed from Shawn. He wrote a story titled "Kid Rabbit," about a rabbit detective who solved dastardly crimes. This story was a huge success and was soon followed by "Kid Fox," "Kid Alligator," "Kid Koala," "Kid Mouse," and "Kid Comet." I joined in, writing "Kid Dragon."

As I publish their writing, I teach a skill or two in the conventions of print. I find that skills taught in a meaningful context are well retained by my students, and they are usually able to apply them as they encounter new situations in their reading and writing. As I edit "Kid Fox," I talk with Jake about capitalizing the words of the title and using exclamation marks. With Jerry's longer piece, a seven-page mystery, we work on paragraph organization, color coding sentences that belong together in a paragraph. After one child's writing had been edited several times using this approach, he handed me a draft with the comment, "This time I tried to keep all the pink stuff together and all the blue and green together . . . ."

Because progress seen in a special education classroom is not always reflected in student performance on standardized testing, I have learned to look very carefully for progress in my children. Sometimes jumps in achievement are remarkable. But most often, progress is slow, quiet, subtle—so easy to miss. I look to see if the letter/sound associations I am teaching are showing up in the child's writing. I look at the child's writing over time to see where the child stands in the progression from early to more mature writing. I look for clues in a child's writing as to whether she is taking things from other print environments and using them in her own writing. Are conventions appearing? How is the child reading? Is the child developing new, reliable reading strategies? Is the child making meaning out of the printed word?

Mostly, I ask myself, does this child feel good about himself as a reader, writer, learner? Does this child feel successful? Does this child see reading and writing as a joy, not a task? If I can answer yes to these questions, I know that the child is making progress, no matter how subtle. And whether the children progress by leaps or quiet steps, it is my job to keep reading and writing delays from becoming terminal. As I lead, stretch, demonstrate, and teach, it is my job to stand steadfastly behind the children, sometimes shouting, sometimes whispering, "Yes, yes you can."

Until they do!

References

Anderson, Richard C., E. H. Hiebert, J. A. Scott, and I. A. Wilkinson. 1984. *Becoming a Nation of Readers.* Washington, DC: National Institute of Education.

Arthur, Robert. 1967. *The Three Investigators Mystery Series.* New York: Random House.

Cleary, Beverly. 1965. *The Mouse and the Motorcycle.* New York: Dell.

Furnas, Alfreda B. 1985. "Watch Me." In *Breaking Ground: Teachers Relate Reading and Writing in the Elementary School,* edited by Jane Hansen, Thomas Newkirk, and Donald H. Graves. Portsmouth, NH: Heinemann.

Hansen, Jane. 1987. *When Writers Read.* Portsmouth, NH: Heinemann.

Newkirk, Thomas. 1989. *More than Stories: The Range of Children's Writing.* Portsmouth, NH: Heinemann.

Wilder, Laura I. 1935. *Little House on the Prairie.* New York: Harper and Row.

2. A Journey to Meaning

Marie Dionisio

Every year for the past four years, it's been the same. Middle school remedial reading students come into my room expecting the same workbooks and skills exercises that they've had in the past. Every year I begin by explaining that they won't be getting any workbooks this year, that we'll each be choosing what we'd like to read, that we'll be talking together about books and reading, and that by sharing together we'll be helping each other to become better readers. And every year their reactions are the same: disbelief, guarded interest, uncertainty, but ultimately, a willingness to give it a chance.

So begins our journey. It is not an easy road; rather it is rutted and uneven. But travel has its own reward. For me, it's the voices of real readers. For the kids, it's the enthusiasm and confidence they develop.

In September, kids tell me that they do not read on their own and that they do not enjoy reading. Most of them think people read only because "they have to" and the good readers are "the ones who don't make any mistakes." I have come to understand from my students that remedial readers do not view reading as "the act of meaning construction," in the words of Gordon Wells (1986). My students do not read when they come to my class because they see no meaning in it. Reading is neither meaningful to their lives nor something they can make sense of when they attempt it. My initial challenge each year is to help them discover the notion of reading as meaning making, to break down their performance view of reading and their reliance (long drilled) on strategies that "make nonsense out of what should be sense" (Smith 1985, 6).

I meet with the remedial readers in my sixth-, seventh-, and eighth-grade classes on three consecutive days out of a six-day cycle during the school year. Classroom procedures are modeled on Atwell's (1987) reading workshop. Each day they choose their own books from a variety of sources and read for extended amounts of time in class. They are required to write at least one journal letter per cycle. Every class begins with a five-minute minilesson, during which I focus on the strategies good readers use, present book and author talks, and model my own response to the adolescent novels I read (Atwell 1987).

The vehicle

The first leg of our journey requires a change of vehicle, replacing isolated reading skills with the strategies real readers use. This is accomplished through minilessons that demonstrate these strategies as alternatives. No matter what strategies I discuss, my primary focus remains making sense of text, because as Frank Smith (1985) says, "Reading directly for meaning . . . becomes the best strategy for reading, not a consequence of reading words and letters, but an alternative" (111).

I begin by convincing kids that they know a great deal about how language works and that they can rely on that knowledge to help them read. I discuss the limitations that short-term memory imposes on the reading process. I follow this with minilessons on grouping words with the eyes to chunk meaning and stopping the eyes on important, meaningful words. Next come discussions on how context is used to predict words and how constant rereading interferes with meaning. When and why readers abandon books is the subject of another minilesson. I also do one that explains how long-term memory assists us in predicting words as we read by using our accumulated knowledge of how language works. This series of minilessons concludes with a summary lesson highlighting the habits that interfere with reading and hints to improve reading. My strategy minilessons are based on the work of Frank Smith (1985).

Reading too slowly seems to be the most common and, indeed, the biggest impediment to making meaning from text for my remedial readers. For many students, this is caused by sounding out words as the first strategy for reading, moving the lips, subvocalizing, pointing to words, and other word-by-word reading strategies. Each of these not only slows readers down but actually interferes with meaning (Smith 1985). For this reason, we talk a great deal about reading faster, as fast as we can. And we return to this issue over and over throughout the year.

Reading faster surfaces as the first strategy students mention to me in journal letters. They are usually amazed when reading faster helps them understand more; to them it seems counter to logic.

Dear Ms. D,
    I tried reading faster and it worked really good. I read about 25 pages today. I didn't talk and didn't move my lips. I understood everything. I didn't think it would work, but it did!

Gail

Dear Ms. D,
    I'm so into *Mr Popper's Penguins.* I love this book a lot. Now I know why this is a Newberry Award book. Today I read 26 pages in 25 minets.

Your friend,
Janis

The kids seem to notice on their own that the new strategies are not the only aids to faster reading and understanding more. They seem to catch on to the positive effects of reading books they really like.

Well Ms. D,

I'm reading alot faster because of your little talks and also you said, "When you like a book you read it faster" and that's what I did. I liked the book I was reading so much even when I am working and then I get a 15 minute break, I go downstairs and read for those 15 minutes. I just want to say thank you for showing me reading can be fun too.

Sally

Ms. D,

I am so proud of myself. I finished the book *[Sooner or Later]* in 6 days. That's record time for me! It was a *really* good book.

Toni

The terrain

Three of these letters suggest another aspect of our journey, the terrain. The kids' positive comments about the books they read may seem to be an aside, but in actuality, they are as important as the new reading strategies. Finding books they really like enables the kids to change their reading strategies. The freedom, and indeed encouragement, to abandon books they don't like is essential. If kids can't freely try out books, it is unlikely they'll discover books they really like. Those students who continually abandon books do not adopt new reading strategies as quickly as those who find books they love early on.

Observing contrasts such as this convinces me of the importance of the terrain—the books kids choose—especially for the remedial reader. My classroom shelves are filled with books written expressly for adolescents, books that deal with situations, concerns, and feelings with which my kids can identify. It is interesting to note that the vast majority of these books are written well above what would be called the reading levels of my remedial students as determined by standardized tests. This phenomenon is supported by Richard Anderson and his colleagues at the Center for the Study of Reading (University of Illinois). They report that student interest in reading materials has an effect that is thirty times greater than readability in determining the student's capacity to read those materials (1984, 24).

Early in the year, I introduce a wide range of books that are sure to have high appeal for my students. In these minilessons, I talk about a particular book or author I have enjoyed. I give a brief description of the story and read aloud a carefully chosen excerpt. I end with my personal response to the book. Besides introducing kids to good books, these minilessons model the way a good reader talks about books and authors.

I choose books for book talks from as wide a variety as possible. I want to find something to appeal to everyone. My choices include such books as *Where the Red Fern Grows,* by Wilson Rawls, *A Bundle of Sticks,* by Pat Rhoades Mauser, *The Lion, the Witch, and the Wardrobe,* by C. S. Lewis, *The Last Mission,* by Harry Mazer, *This Place Has No Atmosphere,* by Paula Danziger, *A Day No Pigs Would Die,* by Robert Newton Peck, *Gentlehands,* by M. E. Kerr, and *Say Hello to the Hitman,* by Jay Bennett. Being able to talk with honest enthusiasm about a large number of adolescent novels is crucial. It provides kids with a basis for choosing and reading books successfully.

Sally's comment, "I'm reading faster . . . you said, 'When you like a book you read it faster' and that's what I did," is proof enough. Would changes occur if I chose books for them? I don't think so. In the beginning, they don't trust my choices. In the past, they've rarely liked what teachers gave them to read. They need the opportunity to choose for themselves, to freely abandon books they don't like, and to discover ones they do like before they'll consider my suggestions. Early journal letters usually report book titles and whether or not they are good. The books in the following letters were chosen by the kids without recommendations from anyone. In fact, I've never read either book.

Dear Ms. D,
    I finished *When the Boys Ran the House.* I really liked it. It was a super book.
                                                                    Gary

Dear Ms. D,
    The book im reading is called *The Secrets of the Shopping Mall.* I like this book becuse it's a mistary and I love spooky storys. This book is very intresting becuse it's about this girl named Teresa and this boy named Barnie and there in a shopping mall and they hear alot of noises. As I read on I get more scared of shopping malls but there's no way I'm going to stop shopping. And I'm not going to stop reading this book!
                                                                    Jane

The fuel

Initial success with reading prods them to continue the journey, but the dialogue journals provide the real fuel, powering an ever-improving vehicle over unknown terrain. The journals allow these kids to try out their meanings on an interested fellow reader, looking for reassurance, confirmation, new directions for thinking, or simply someone who really listens to what they say. It's these conversations, exemplifying the social nature of reading, that propel these readers to the journey's end.

Every year, I learn something more about the importance of journal conversation for remedial readers. I frequently ask students if they like the journals and why. The response is overwhelmingly positive. The reasons given vary widely, yet always cause me to reflect on the impact of our letters and on the effectiveness of journal dialogue as an agent for change.

Joey said, "I like 'em cause you get a response." "I get to express my feelings and see what you and other people feel about their books," answered Jimmy. Alice and Gail remarked, "When you write to me about your book, that's what I like."

My kids have taught me the importance of my talking with them as an interested fellow reader rather than as a teacher. The purpose of my letters is to have individual conversations with each reader about books, characters, and reading strategies. I never write a letter with a preplanned agenda. All my letters to kids are my real responses to the issues they raise in their letters. I agree with their opinion of a book; I disagree and give a reason for my opinion. I confirm what they say about a reading strategy, or I suggest one that might solve a problem they are having. I suggest books that I think they might like, and I tell them about the book I am reading.

"How's your book?" is the question kids ask most frequently in their letters. I always answer with my personal response to the book I'm reading. The frequency of this request made me realize the importance of my increasing familiarity with and appreciation of good adolescent literature. As Nancie Atwell (1987) said, "Living the literature becomes possible for students when teachers live the literature, too" (200). I read with my students during class time. If I don't read, they don't read. The importance of being a visible reading model can't be stressed enough. Intrinsic in the question "How's your book?" is the kid's knowledge that I am reading a book all the time.

Dear Ms. D,
    I did give *Just Between Us* a little longer. And now I'm really into it. Its good. This year this class has really got me into reading. I think over the vacation I'll read *Truth or Dare*. *Just Between Us* has parts were I feel I had those problems or told somebody a secret and they didn't keep it. I'm on the 5th chapter and its good. I don't want to stop reading it. The title *Truth or Dare* makes me wonder what the book is going to be about. And I like that in a book. How's your book?
                                                                                    Gail

Dear Gail,
    I also saw some of my problems from when I was your age in both *Just Between Us* and *Truth or Dare*. I think in both books the problems are very common ones; lots of people have similar experiences. You're right about the title, *Truth or Dare*. It does make you wonder what the book is going to be about. I always wonder what a book will be about from its title. I think that's fun!
    I'm reading *Where the Red Fern Grows,* by Wilson Rawls. It's an excellent book. It's about a boy on a farm and how he gets, trains, and loves two coon hounds. The boy and the dogs grow together, and the strong bond that holds them also holds me to the book. Rawls is a wonderful writer. I love the way he puts words together.
    You've really changed as a reader. You should be very proud of yourself. You have taken some real risks, like trying to read faster, giving books more of a chance, and pretending to be the main character. Those risks have been worth it! Your letter tells me that you are really inside the books you're reading. I think it's great.
                                                                                    Ms. D

As journal letters inform me that the kids are beginning to read faster, understand what they read, and discover books they enjoy, I want them to find ways to get inside the stories they read. To nudge them, I direct my minilessons to a different kind of reading strategy. I discuss strategies such as imagining yourself as the main character, predicting what will happen next, identifying the conflict in a story, comparing story events or character emotions to your own experiences, and noticing how main characters change.

When I discuss a new strategy in a minilesson, I often end with an invitation:

Today in your reading, try to put yourself in the main character's place. Think about what you would do in the same situation. See if you can feel the character's feelings. When reading time is over, write to me in your journal and tell me what happened.

Invitations like this do not always result in student letters about the strategy discussed in the minilesson. Talk about reading strategies is most often student-initiated rather than in response to my questions or invitations. Their remarks are about things they've tried as readers. In many cases, they seem to want confirmation or reassurance, or they express surprise. On occasion, I initiate reading strategy dialogues as a result of something I've observed or heard during oral sharing.

The personal and conversational nature of the journal breaks down the traditional teacher-student barrier. The absence of this barrier makes my letters about reading strategies more in the nature of suggestions from one reader to another than of teacher directives. What's more, these suggestions are taken into consideration by the reader, who has the option of accepting or rejecting them.

The following excerpt occurred after I suggested to Alice that she try to keep her mind from wandering while she reads:

Dear Ms. D,
Today I tried to focus on the story. It worked out pretty good. But I still have to work on it.

Alice

Dear Alice,
I'm impressed by what you said in your letter. Focusing your mind on the story as you read is an important reading strategy. I'm also impressed because you said you still have to work on it. Recognizing the ways in which you want to change as a reader is an important sign that proves you have already changed! Keep it up.

Ms. D

In the next exchange it seems as if my comment "You could be right" is the key Jimmy needs to continue using prediction as he reads *Dracula, Go Home.*

Dear Ms. D,
I am reading *Dracula Go Home.* It is about a boy named Larry and he was on his way to his aunt's hotel. On his way he cut through the graveyard and he see Dracula. He ran to his aunt's hotel. No one was after him. He went in and saw his aunt and said I came to help you for my vacation. Later in the day Dracula came in and wanted room 13. He got it. He never came down to eat. I think he is a robber or a killer or he is after something in that room.

Jimmy

Dear Jimmy,
You could be right! Why do you think he is a robber or a killer or after something in that room?

Ms. D

Dear Ms. D,
I think he is a robber because every year he askes for the same room like there is rubbies or dimins that Larry's aunt is finding in that room and he knows that it is in that room somewhere. I think he is might be a killer because he is dressed in black.

Jimmy

Dear Jimmy,
You're doing a great job of sorting out the author's clues in *Dracula, Go Home.* Sorting out clues and making predictions about what will happen or who is doing what are the reasons I really love to read mysteries.

Ms. D

Dear Ms. D,
    Thanks for the good news about the book.

Jimmy

Jimmy's final letter tells me that my talk about strategies was seen by him as an affirmation that asking himself questions as he reads is a good reading strategy.

    Talk about strategies is not confined to teacher-student dialogues but creeps into the letters kids write to each other during the second half of each year.

Dear Alice,
    When you start a chapter in that book [*Just As Long As We're Together*], try to finish it the same day. I think you will really like it. So how is it. What is your favorite part so far? I had so many favorite parts. Try to read next week when we have no school.

Gail

Dear Gail,
    I am gona read it next week and a little every night in the week. My favorite part is chapter 4, Rachel's Room because it's funny.

Alice

It is easy to hear the conversation of real friends, equals engaged in a mutually interesting activity.

    Excitement about books and reading grows, and with it the confidence of my remedial readers. The more they read, the more they share, the greater their excitement and confidence become. By spring these kids notice they're reading the same books as their nonremedial peers, and some even suggest books to friends in "advanced" classes.

    During the final weeks of one school year, a visitor came into a remedial reading class. Seeing three sixth-grade girls talking excitedly and writing, each one on her own sheet of paper, she asked me what they were doing. I responded, "Why don't you ask them; they'll be happy to tell you." She did, and was amazed when they said, "Oh, we're making a list of books that we want to read over the summer." Before the visitor knew it, she was making a list of books that the kids suggested!

The map

The successes of my remedial students over the last four years, especially as compared to my remedial readers of the past, convince me of the validity of the reading workshop as an avenue to reading improvement. Never before did I see remedial readers develop the reading habit.

    Reading workshop provides my students with new terrain to travel, a well-equipped vehicle to drive, and the fuel to power it. But how do they navigate? What guides their way? As I reflect on my experiences with and observations of these kids, I think a lot about what made it possible. My modeling and patience emerge as the map that guides my remedial students along their journey. This map provides them not only with alternative routes but with the freedom to choose their own road at each fork.

Throughout the year, I model my own reading process. I do this when I talk about a book or strategy in a minilesson, when I write a journal letter, when I speak during oral sharing at the end of class, and anytime I talk with kids about books or reading. And I encourage the kids to talk in the same way. Truly, I have become just one member of the community of readers in my classroom.

Perhaps the most important lesson I've learned from my students is that teaching is an exercise in patience. Changes in human behavior never happen quickly. This is especially true for remedial readers. Just as I give my kids real time in class for reading, I am conscious of allowing them the real time they need to experiment and to change as readers.

In June, I ask students to write me a final journal letter about how they have changed as readers. Here's what four of them said last year:

The way my reading changed is that in fifth grade we had to read out of this book that I hated. Now in sixth grade, we got to pick our own book and read it and we don't have to do any comprehension sheets or work in the workbooks. I think if you wanna be a good reader, you have to read books that you like, not books that other people like. Also in reading, we have journals that we write to the teacher or somebody in the class. The things that we talk about in our journals are about our book, if we like it and things like that.

I changed my reading a couple of ways this year. I don't move my lips anymore and that helps me read a lot faster. We have a minilesson every time we read, and those helped me a lot. I like in Ms. D's class how if we don't like the book we're reading, we could just drop the book and start a new one. We don't have to do comprehensions or anything like that. Instead we write in our journals to the other classmates or we write to Ms. D and tell her all about our book. And she writes back and tells us all about her book. I share my ideas with Ms. D and she shares hers with me. well, I really, really think I changed a lot.

The way I changed as a reader is that I read a lot faster. I like to read on my own also. I never knew how much fun reading can be. I really like conflicts the most in a book. Some leads are really dull so I think you should give a book 20 pages before you stop reading it. Last year I didn't read on my own that much and I read slower. I also stopped reading a book if I didn't like the lead. That is the way I changed as a reader.

I enjoyed this class, but it's time for us kids to move on. You must be the best teacher in this hole school because you can teach a person only by writing and reading; the first day I ever got to this class I didn't belive it. I have learn a lot, I've learn how to read faster, how I could understand the story and many thing. I really enjoy being here. THANK YOU!

The same kids who arrived in my class hating reading now speak with the authority of real readers. They suggest books to friends, visit the library regularly, make lists of books they'll read next, and talk incessantly to anyone who will listen about the *best* book they just read. And so a year's journey ends, for the kids and for me. Each of us may have taken a different road and traveled in a slightly different vehicle, but we've arrived at the same destination. Every one of us has changed as a reader, and as a learner.

References

Anderson, Richard C., Jana Mason, and Larry Shirey. 1984. "The Reading Group: An Experimental Investigation of a Labyrinth." *Reading Research Quarterly* 20 (Fall):6–38.

Atwater, Richard and Florence. 1956. *Mr. Popper's Penguins*. New York: Dell.

Atwell, Nancie. 1987. *In the Middle: Writing, Reading, and Learning with Adolescents*. Portsmouth, NH: Boynton/Cook.

Bennett, Jay. 1981. *Say Hello to the Hitman*. New York: Dell.

Blume, Judy. 1987. *Just As Long As We're Together*. New York: Dell.

Carris, Joan. 1982. *When the Boys Ran the House*. New York: Dell.

Danziger, Paula. 1986. *This Place Has No Atmosphere*. New York: Dell.

Hart, Bruce and Carole. 1978. *Sooner or Later*. New York: Avon Books.

Kerr, M. E. 1978. *Gentlehands*. New York: Bantam Books.

Lewis, C. S. 1950. *The Lion, the Witch and the Wardrobe*. New York: Macmillan.

Mauser, Pat Rhodes. 1982. *A Bundle of Sticks*. New York: Macmillan.

Mazer, Harry. 1979. *The Last Mission*. New York: Dell.

Peck, Richard. 1979. *The Secrets of the Shopping Mall*. New York: Dell.

Peck, Robert Newton. 1972. *A Day No Pigs Would Die*. New York: Dell.

Pfeffer, Susan Beth. 1980. *Just Between Us*. New York: Dell.

———. 1983. *Truth or Dare*. New York: Scholastic.

Platt, Kin. 1979. *Dracula, Go Home*. New York: Dell.

Rawls, Wilson. 1961. *Where the Red Fern Grows*. New York: Bantam Books.

Smith, Frank. 1985. *Reading without Nonsense*. New York: Teacher's College Press.

Wells, Gordon. 1986. *The Meaning Makers: Children Learning Language and Using Language to Learn*. Portsmouth, NH: Heinemann.

3. Interrogating Silences

Esther Sokolov Fine

Sylvie was a tall, white girl with black hair, of French Acadian descent, in the sixth grade. Although some French was spoken in her home, her first language was English. She had repeated one grade during her early primary years in another province. She had severe emotional difficulties that showed up both at home and in the regular classroom.

The oldest of three girls, Sylvie lived with both parents. Her father worked on road construction; her mother did not work outside the home. The family lived in the low-rise section of the inner-city housing project immediately behind the school and received rent subsidy, disability insurance, and a family allowance. Sylvie was the cousin of a five-year-old boy who some years earlier had been murdered by his own mother (Sylvie's aunt, her father's sister). The aunt, back in society after only three years, had the legal right to visit her other children at certain times. Sylvie's parents were helping to look after these children, and it was in Sylvie's home that the visits took place.

Sylvie had been receiving special education support for a period of four years. Before entering my program, she had been receiving learning-center support for several periods per day (the learning-center time had gradually been increased over the years). The regular classroom teacher reported improvement in her behavior over the course of the school year and told of satisfactory performance in the arts, language, and environmental studies portion of the program. He reported her as still having difficulty in mathematics, French, and physical education. Sylvie had a reputation in the school for being disruptive and subject to uncontrolled outbursts in which she would throw classroom furniture and scream at the teacher. In my learning disabilities program she showed herself capable of reasonable behavior and excellent performance in reading and writing.

Sylvie was one of nine inner-city special education students, aged nine to fourteen, who collaboratively composed a dramatic text in my classroom. As they worked together, many of their conflicts emerged and were taken up, and the students gradually moved from almost paralyzed silence to creative interaction. This story gives us glimpses into worlds that children often remain silent about in the classroom. Their silence can result in forms of isolation that make school learning almost impossible for some.

In my classroom, I explored possibilities for unlocking the silence that exists for such students, so that school could become relevant, hospitable, and stimulating. For four days, I tape-recorded a series of collaborative text-production sessions at a round table. Students were asked to determine a theme, a plot, and characters for their drama. They were asked to decide who they wanted to be and were encouraged to play more than one role. I hoped that by playing several roles they would experience transformations and make discoveries about themselves and each other. Through a series of personal decisions and struggles for voice and authority in our group drama, Sylvie gradually came to play a very key role.

The project

During a long and frustrating series of practice sessions, the students resisted the possibility of a project. They tested and teased until they felt safe enough to take the personal risks involved in role-play. They needed to make certain that racist remarks and other forms of victimization and embarrassment would be dealt with fairly at the table. One happy day, following many weeks of such sessions and an extensive search for the common ground of a text on which we could all comfortably collaborate, two of our boys, Clyde and Ronnie, brought a sample text from their regular classroom, which they had worked on with several other students. This text was actually a script for a video drama they had helped create and was based on a TV show. These boys read out and tape-recorded their script in my room, and it served as the necessary inspiration for our project. The other students listened carefully as the two rehearsed and taped their script. In an instant, the students discovered "TV script" as their common ground for dramatic collaboration. "Can we do one, too?" came their chorus of voices. They had found their medium at last.

We dashed to the round table, sat down, turned on the tape recorder, and I asked two questions: "What do you want the play to be about?" and "Who do you want to be?" There followed four sessions over a period of four days. The themes they chose for their drama were prostitution, drugs, and drinking. A loose version of Miami Vice became the "location" for a story filled with content that was familiar to children from this part of the city.

The initial session began as a fantasy play, with quick agreement among all present as to what the themes would be. It developed into a patriarchal text in which the boys created their own roles as well as most of the roles for the girls. The girls, assigned to mainly victim characters, managed to modify their roles somewhat and sidestep the most obvious victim positions, but never really moved outside of the boy-text that was established at the outset.

The original plot unfolded approximately as follows: One dark night, in a neighborhood where there are lots of prostitutes, pimps, drugs, and drinking, a young prostitute is murdered in a dark alley. The murder is committed by her pimp, who is disguised as a woman. The murder is witnessed by a bag lady who, though observed by the murderer, manages to escape. The pimp hires a hitman to kill the bag lady. The bag lady, knowing this, bravely goes to the police with her story. The body of the young prostitute, whose name is Lady Love, is mysteriously discovered the next morning in bed in a room at the neighborhood shelter for women. Lady Love's unsuspecting best friend, Seashell, comes to the shelter that morning to meet Lady Love. The two of them have planned to escape from their life of prostitution, and from their pimp, and head for Los Angeles. When she arrives, Seashell is told by Tricia, who runs the shelter, that her friend is dead. Although she is in shock, she decides to run away before the police arrive and question her. She escapes over the back fence. There is a police chase. She manages to get away, but a piece of her red dress tears off on the fence and remains as evidence.

Figure 3–1 is an illustration of the police chase produced by Jackie, who decided to take on the role of a police artist. He labored over his drawing, directing us to it often as a reference point and a source of truth during remaining sessions.

Figure 3–1

Jackie's police chase illustration.

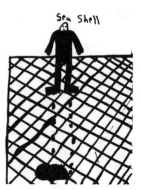

The students produced quite a few police characters. Some were double agents who attempted to entrap criminals by pretending to buy drugs on the street. They had names like Crab, Fish, and Bruce. Sylvie took on the role of a policewoman disguised as a prostitute, who propositions men and then arrests them. There was even a character named Big Bad Billy Joe, played by Craig, the weakest member of our group. Craig wanted his character to be another murderer disguised as a "nice guy." He had a great deal of difficulty fitting himself into the story, but with a few twists of logic, he managed to have a moment near the end where he was the acknowledged murderer, although the actual murder scene was never played out. All significant male roles were roles of power created by the boys themselves. Most of the female roles were victim roles created by the boys, accepted and then modified somewhat by the girls. There was a great deal of competition for the police roles. No one wanted to play the pimp. Sylvie reluctantly played the dead body in the opening scene. Melissa played the murdered woman's best friend, Seashell, while Sylvie maneuvered her way out of the victim position to become various incidental characters, and finally the very powerful bag lady, who has seen and knows all. Jackie, Ronnie, and Clyde played police characters. Our educational assistant played Tricia, who ran the women's shelter. Mark, our star athlete and struggling reader/writer, appointed himself "director" and invented the murder scene, the pimp, and the bag lady. He did not take on a role. I played a ninety-four-year-old woman who lived alone and was quite dependent on neighbors and police.

Initially, two distinctly different ideas for opening scenes were proposed: (1) the body of a dead prostitute is found in a women's shelter, and (2) two policemen, partners in the same division, who have met by accidentally entrapping each other in a drug bust on the street, are having tea and cheeseburgers in a restaurant that is run by a drug dealer. What followed was the production of a large number of experimental characters. Some were sustained in later sessions, others were modified or dropped entirely. The exact order of events in this opening scene was never fully decided. As the narrative unfolded, all of the events in both versions were apparently assumed to have taken place at the very beginning. The exact sequence never became a troublesome issue, although it was never firmly established.

Sylvie

At the outset, Sylvie wanted to be "nobody." There was a point very early in the first session when Sylvie succumbed to group pressure. She said, "Ok, I'll be the prostitute, too." This was a very important moment, for it was here that Sylvie decided that it was safe to be the dead prostitute, perhaps because of the invention of the women's shelter, which in the story provided a safe context in which to play such an awful role. Perhaps, too, it was safe because the prostitute's troubles and suffering were over, given that she's already dead when the story opens. Once the group had fulfilled its quest for a victim, the drama seemed able to continue in a new way. When she said, "I'll be the prostitute, *too,"* Sylvie meant that she was beginning to develop a notion of alternatives for herself in this text, and that she could now handle the responsibility and opportunity of playing more than one character. She was willing to play the already dead victim, proposed in the opening scene, at least partly because she saw that playing this victim role did not lock her permanently into a victim position. And I think she saw that a volunteer victim was what was needed to finally get this drama going.

By deciding to play the body of the dead prostitute, Lady Love, Sylvie acknowledged her own private nightmare. She's the victim. Like her young cousin in real life, she's dead. But so many other characters were produced that Sylvie found the opportunity to play a range of other interesting roles. She seemed to see the power potential in characters the minute they were created, and she developed an array of strong female characters for herself. The two most significant of these were an undercover policewoman who posed as a prostitute and made arrests, and the bag lady/witness. Sylvie seemed willing to represent the victim position for the sake of getting the drama going, but she was never willing in this project, even symbolically, to sacrifice herself.

A widespread interest developed as to who would be the bag lady. Melissa and Sylvie were both contenders. Sylvie had helped to develop the bag lady character and had worked hard to maneuver herself into that role. Melissa, who arrived late from another class, had joined in eagerly. They were the only girls present. This was the first female character that seemed to have significant power. After all, she is the only witness to a murder, and therefore, to a certain extent, she can determine what happens. She is in danger because there is a hitman out to kill her, but on the other hand, she has knowledge and power. She can expose the killer. She knows the pimp because she sees him every night and recognizes him easily at the scene of the crime before she runs away. So she holds most of the cards, unless she gets killed. Both girls wanted to play the bag lady at the moment when it became clear in Mark's version, which everyone present seemed to be accepting, that this character would have so much power. I resolved the problem by giving the role to Sylvie, who had worked hard to carve out the bag lady character for herself. Melissa acquiesced, moving quickly back into one of her more minor roles as undercover cop.

Until this point, the majority of female characters were victims, roles created by the boys and accepted, however willingly or unwillingly, by the girls. The reproduction of gender relations in this drama became staggering to watch, once I began to see it that way. Most of the participants wanted to be cops. Mark wanted to be the director so as to exert power while maintaining enough control over things that no one would ask him to look at print or reveal any weakness or ignorance. Craig wanted to be the murderer and even agreed to play the pimp if that's what he finally had to do in order to be the murderer and have a key and guaranteed part.

Donald Graves, in his work about the writing development of young children (1983), wrote:

Voice is the imprint of ourselves on our writing. It is that part of the self that pushes the writing ahead, the dynamo in the process. Take the voice away and the writing collapses of its own weight. There is no writing, just words following words. Voiceless writing is addressed "to whom it may concern." The voice shows how I choose information, organize it, select the words, all in relation to what I want to say and how I want to say it. The reader says, "someone is here. I know that person. I've been there, too." But the writer's voice is in the right register, not pointing to itself but to the material. The voice is the frame of the window through which the information is seen. (227–28)

But what happens to the student whose knowledge is secret? What about the "ownership" and "authority" of a student who has been carefully taught by experience to keep the window shades drawn? What can a girl like Sylvie do when she has the skills to make herself heard but is not allowed, either by the conventions of traditional schooling or by her family, to talk about what she knows in a public setting? How can she become the authority over her own text? Who will believe her when she cannot back up her opinions with information, not because she does not have the information but because it is too private? Sylvie had a terrible choice to make in a later session, in which she became painfully conscious of her own dilemma.

Sylvie took the supreme risk of revealing a small piece of her most private knowledge and its very painful source. She told us that her aunt was a murderer and that she herself was the group's true authority on the topic of the length of a murder sentence. Sylvie had never been able to function as an authority on this subject before in school, while in fact it was probably the area of personal knowledge she most needed to assert control over. Here, the text production process provided an important moment for her because she could now author the text in a way that helped her begin to formulate her own way of looking at the events that produced her secret and terrible knowledge, and because she could suddenly assume the status of a "knower" in the group during a discussion in which meanings were being hotly disputed. Much of Sylvie's personal knowledge belongs in the category of "secret." It is this type of knowledge that is under most circumstances considered inappropriate for a school setting. In the following passage, students were producing endings for the drama. There was a dispute between Brenda and Sylvie about the length of murder sentences. Here, Sylvie made a space for herself as a knower.

It was Brenda's turn to make up an ending:

Brenda: They have a trial, and the jury find him guilty and all that and they find him guilty and put him in jail.

Esther: For how many years, for life or for what?

Sylvie: Three. [Sylvie's insertion here was very important, insofar as it revealed her intimate knowledge of this fact and because of its power to give her the confidence to continue to assert her knowledge on this topic.]

Brenda: For a life sentence.

Sylvie: No. [Sylvie knows more than Brenda realizes here.]

Brenda: Yes!

Sylvie: For killing somebody? No, you only get three years.

Brenda: Shut up, this is my story, not yours. Ha ha, throw him [in] for life.

Sylvie: No, three years.

Brenda: Hush.

This was a rare example of a dispute between girls in the sessions. Both were asserting: Brenda, her story and her right to make up her own version of it, and Sylvie, her deep, painful, and still secret personal knowledge.

Sylvie: When you kill somebody you only get in trouble for three years.

Brenda: Three years, oh yeah, you wish, three years. [Brenda has completely misunderstood Sylvie here, and Sylvie has not yet offered any of her secret information.]

Sylvie: I know!!! You wanna bet? Three years.

Brenda: You better stop.

Sylvie: Okay, ask my mother, she knows.

Brenda: Three years.

Sylvie: Yeah.

Esther: Okay, so . . .

Sylvie: My aunt was in there for three years.

Brenda: So?

Sylvie: So, she killed somebody. She was only in there for three years.

Brenda: So, not everybody gets in there for three years. Some people get in there longer.

Sylvie: You know, if you kill . . . forget it! You only go for three years, I know that.

Esther: And then what happens after the three years?

Sylvie: He comes out and starts more trouble, so they put him in jail for life.

Brenda: Stupid.

Sylvie: Yeah.

Esther: So it takes two offences, is that what you are saying?

Sylvie: Yeah.

Esther: So, you go in jail, come out, do it again? Or do something again?

Sylvie: Yeah. [Committing a second crime is no doubt what Sylvie and her family fear will happen with the aunt who is on parole with certain visiting rights.]

Brenda did not accept Sylvie's knowledgeable challenge to this set of meanings. Sylvie, on the other hand, had taken the opportunity to put forward her version of a flawed legal system that had left her aunt, a murderer, free to live in the outside world, to visit her children and keep the wider family in a state of ongoing fear and apprehension of what might happen. Sylvie had challenged conventional meaning here, and in challenging Brenda, a strong leader, she had challenged the group. She had chosen to reveal and then to utilize her personal knowledge to shape and then put forward her own strong statement.

The case for dramatic curriculum

James Moffett (1983) makes a strong case for the use of drama as a means of activating student voices and interaction in the classroom. He describes drama as

the most accessible form of literature for young and uneducated people. It is made up of action; and the verbal action is of a sort we all practice all the time. A kindergarten child or an older illiterate can soliloquize and converse, verbalize to himself and vocalize to others. No written symbols are required. Drama is primitive: not only does it hit us at the level of sensation, affect, and conditioned response, but it seems in all cultures to be virtually the first, if not *the* first, verbal art to come into being because it is oral and behavioral and functional, evolving out of real-life activities. (63–64)

My goal was to make transformative moments possible for the students. The project was a pedagogical exploration intended to generate and support students in a struggle with multiple and contradictory meanings in which they would have the possibility to form new meanings and new visions of whom they could become (Simon 1987).

This project, filled with voices and stories that want to be heard, has a wider story to tell about the politics of silence, about the power relations involved in schooling, and about the effects of pervasive social violence on many inner-city, female, and minority children. A skeletal version is told here, as a demonstration, in the hope that teachers will explore new ways of encouraging the emergence of unusual voices and stories in their classrooms. Preserving the silences of children who are "different" can be as damaging as forcing children to expose their secrets when they are not ready. Teachers need to know students well enough to help them build safe bridges that will enable them to find their voices in the classroom and in the world, however "different" and painful their stories may be.

Students in this project moved carefully from silence into a type of exchange that allowed for the production of meaning that is part of our learning to be literate and competent language users. The project contributed to the students' confidence and to their ability to work together to share ideas and interrogate one another's worlds. They found themselves able to develop collaboratively a complex narrative in which there were spaces for inserting their individual worlds and visions. They talked, they wrote, and they drew many illustrations as their narrative grew. Their interaction turned them into playwrights. Their voluminous and complex text engrossed and astonished them as they discovered their own and other voices in very profound ways.

References

Graves, Donald H. 1983. *Writing: Teachers and Children at Work*. Portsmouth, NH: Heinemann.

Moffett, James. 1983. *Teaching the Universe of Discourse*. New York: Houghton Mifflin.

Simon, Roger. 1987. "Empowerment as a Pedagogy of Possibility." *Language Arts* 64:370–382.

4. Read Aloud

Ilene Seeman Johnson

It began as a typical morning in a typical middle school special education classroom. My seventh- and eighth-grade students were working on their independent contract assignments. They were using a variety of materials, the "high-interest" type involving the nine subskills of reading. I was catching up with a student, checking his work, and reassigning tasks in relation to his diagnosed needs. It was a successful program with elements of creativity and motivation. Something was missing, however. There was no excitement.

Just as I finished with my student, a carton of paperbacks I had ordered for my classroom arrived. These books were a collection of novels, none of which I had read. Some were suggested by a colleague, based on lists from Nancie Atwell (1987), while others were suggested by avid readers elsewhere. I found myself losing concentration, eyeing the carton. I could not resist. I ripped open the box. Here were one hundred books I had never read, and I was thrilled. I instructed the students to continue with their work. Meanwhile, I was like a child opening up a Christmas gift.

After a few minutes the students got out of their seats, one by one, leaving their high-interest materials behind. David kept watching me and trying to make small talk about the titles. He said, "Any Encyclopedia Brown books? Did you order *About David,* by Pfeffer? What's that one in your hand? Can I just see the one next to you?" Before long, we were all sitting on the floor and leaning over the carton, pulling out books, passing them back and forth, reading the backs aloud. I showed the class *Watership Down,* by Richard Adams, and shyly told them it was about rabbits. The girls dove into the Sweet Valley High collection, while the boys passed back and forth the adventure and mystery books. My super athlete, Tony, grabbed *Ice Magic,* by Matt Christopher, and began reading it on the floor. The room was in disarray, the books were everywhere, and kids were signing out their selections on the blackboard. I was elated. The idea of keeping quiet in the room no longer crossed my mind. The passing on of excitement about books was much more important. I had never seen anything like this in seventeen years of teaching special education.

One of my most apathetic readers, who was stereotyped early in school and programmed to be a "nonreader," called me aside and said, "What happens if I become a bookworm?" The seriousness behind his humor was apparent. Special education youngsters have a "reputation" to uphold. They are "tough, dumb, uninterested children." My students to this day shove books in their coats and hats or give them to other students to carry home for them. They cannot afford to alter the image.

I realized that somehow I had to bring the students back to the basics of beginning reading. What does a mother do when her children are nursery school age? She makes the pilgrimage to the local library to expose her children to the world of books. This is exactly what I did with my daughters Rachel and Jessica. I wanted them to love and be fascinated with books early in their lives. We would sit and look at books, use the computer materials, attend author visits, and talk with the librarians. I created a comfortable experience for the girls. Rachel would practice writing her name at home knowing that, once she could write it legibly, a library card would be issued in her own name. I still smile remembering her proud face on that wonderful day. I followed the same procedure with Jessica eight years later. Our only disagreement would be over my rule "No more than seven books out at a time." We compromised at ten. Jessie now has her library card safely tucked away in her Barbie vault.

I contacted the librarian and made arrangements to have my class visit the library. We were given the royal tour. The students were surprised to find the librarians helpful and interested in their becoming readers. It was revealing to me that over 80 percent of my class did not have individual library cards. This fact reinforced for me that my students were deprived readers as opposed to nonreaders.

Once again, I tried to remember when my daughters were little. We took weekly visits to the library, we belonged to book clubs, and we often spent time at bookstores skimming and purchasing the latest book of our favorite authors. I read constantly to them. Some books were read over and over again. They would always have favorite stories, such as "Three Billy Goats Gruff." They would memorize the book and read aloud with me, echoing my sound, expression, and reading techniques. When they could read to themselves, they would imagine themselves as teachers reading to their students. They sounded just like me! They would pause, they would accentuate action, and they would always have a sense of emotion in their voices.

Rachel and Jessica had modeled their approach to reading after mine. Instead of explaining to them how to read, I showed them. Instead of giving them worksheets on isolated skills, I demonstrated how reading happens. Most importantly, they decided on their own that reading was going to be part of their lives. Once I connected what I had done at home with Rachel and Jessica to my students in the classroom, my approach was simple. I decided to read aloud. Later on I discovered Jim Trelease's (1985) advocacy of reading aloud to children of all ages.

My "read-aloud" program began with S. E. Hinton's *The Outsiders*. I was able to borrow multiple copies, and we dove into the book. The room was silent except for the sound of my voice reading and thirteen pages turning simultaneously. The students read through me, following my voice. They heard and saw at the same time my reading techniques of phrasing, pacing, skimming, and repeating. I did not stop at words they could not define. They either understood the meaning through context or not at all. I paused at places I wished to reflect on and opened the group up to discussions regarding the characters or story interpretation. Often, we debated a decision reached by a character, and I listened to their feelings. We thought about various other options and pretended we were Ponyboy, Johnny, or Dallas. We tried understanding the action of a character from what we read. Often, it was necessary to go back into the book and find passages to support our opinions.

We were totally captivated with the book. We put people who came into the room on hold and ignored the bell system. When we were up to a "great part," we substituted further reading for other subjects. Little distracted us from our reading. Everyone was together; everyone's mind was on the book.

One day, I was reading the part in *The Outsiders* where Ponyboy is at the hospital. His brothers, Sodapop and Darry, are waiting to find out if he is going to be all right. Another character, Johnny, has been seriously injured. It was an extremely emotional part because the three brothers express their love for one another. We had been waiting for at least 100 pages for these characters to admit their true feelings. I felt a lump in my throat, and my eyes filled with tears. I tried to fight the tears and push them back so I could continue to read. Finally, I had to stop. I got off the reading stool, went to my desk to get a tissue, and wiped my eyes. Fran quietly asked, "Are you crying?" I nodded. The room was quiet again. Finally, Robert said, "I could cry myself." Others nodded. The moment was magical, and I will remember it for the rest of my teaching career. We were bonded through reading.

On the final day of reading *The Outsiders,* the students opted to be late for lunch in order to complete the novel. As we reluctantly closed our covers, all fourteen of us were disappointed about ending our reading experience. At the beginning of our next reading session, I explained that *The Outsiders* was a phenomenal book. Although we had finished it, I promised to find others that they would love and relate to on different levels. As Johnny told Ponyboy in the novel, "Nothing gold can stay." We moved on.

I began a quest to find other books we could get lost in together. I wanted to expose them to different walks of life, to particular character developments, and to writing modes such as humor, adventure, and fantasy. *Killing Mr. Griffin,* by Lois Duncan, is another novel that offered tremendous possibilities for character interpretation and understanding peer pressure. The story revolves around high school students who are manipulated by a psychopathic boy who is able to use each student's vulnerability to his advantage. They kidnap their English teacher, who dies accidentally. This novel allowed my readers to imagine they were a part of the story. They were able to analyze the characters and to feel empathy, confusion, and disillusionment. They grew to understand how easily people can be manipulated. At one point Sarah said, "How ridiculous! I would just tell him to do the rest himself and that I wanted out." Other children disagreed with her, using hypothetical examples and real-life situations.

The reading of *Incident at Hawk's Hill,* by Allan Eckert, exposed the students to a different approach. After a few chapters, the class asked to abandon the book. They were overwhelmed by too much lengthy description. Afraid of losing them, I started using the techniques of skimming and skipping. They heard me skip certain passages that were not relevant and go on to reading others that were important to the story. The students were able to follow the storyline involving a young boy and a badger and enjoy their adventure. It isn't likely that any of these children would have selected this book or completed it on their own, but they were pleased to have finished it together.

Read-aloud is one component of my reading program; another is reading workshop. Modeled after Nancie Atwell's (1987) reading workshop, it includes sustained silent reading. In my classroom there is a library that consists of approximately 600 titles including topics such as adventure, humor, sports, mystery, horror, romance, teen life, and animals. The reading level ranges from third grade to adult. The students select books from the library or read books they have chosen elsewhere. No one waits for a bell to ring to begin class. They are eager to have the quiet time to settle in and read. We all read in silence for forty minutes. The most important aspect is that we all read books from adolescent library sources. Again, I am modeling for them. I don't read my adult selections at this time. I'm absorbed in *our* literature, and an honest relationship is established. I do not set myself apart from them or make myself all-knowing.

A third component is the reading journal. This is a written exchange between my students and myself and/or the students themselves on what we are reading. They are permitted to write entries to one another, but I expect to receive at least one entry per week. The entries focus on reactions to plot, character, author intent, style, reading frustrations, reading techniques, and so on. We exchange private thoughts and suggestions through journal entries. Often, the children suggest their own books as read-aloud selections. The students are allowed to question my feelings or reactions to books we have both read during workshop. I allow myself to be vulnerable, and the experience is one of learning for all.

Generally, I allow a one-week interval before we begin the next selection of read-aloud. We need time to digest the novel previously read before moving on to another. During this week we discuss other possible outcomes, read parts over again, and work on individual projects based on the novel. However, the journals are ongoing. I use the journals during read-aloud to work on character development and to demonstrate, for example, how to place yourself in the book. These sophisticated reading skills then get transferred to their journal writings during reading workshop.

I learned not to begin a novel before a vacation because the absence broke our concentration. Occasionally, someone read ahead of the class, but they never minded hearing the part read aloud. If I had to be out of school, the read-aloud would be canceled. Once I had suggested to the substitute to read with the class. When I returned, a spokesperson for the class said, "Please don't have other people read to us. We'd rather wait and have you read to us when you get back. We're used to hearing your voice." Another student said, "The substitute was boring, she didn't stop and let us talk about the book. She didn't change her voice with the different characters. Could you read that part over again?"

During that first year of read-aloud, there were many moments that validated what I was doing in my classroom. Antonio, a boy from an Italian speaking household, stayed after class to speak with me. He said, "Could I borrow the two copies of *Rumble Fish* we have in the library? I am trying to teach my mother to speak English and every night I read aloud to her." I would have bought him the copies! Another girl wrote in her journal,

Dear Mrs. J,

I think my vocabulary is growing. I read much faster now. I feel my eyes move across each line. I'm not afraid of trying any book in the library. Also, sometimes when I talk, I hear myself use words I've never used before. Even my parents noticed I speak differently.

Love,
Marie

In fact, Marie's vocabulary did grow. According to the Iowa Achievement scores, which the district uses to assess reading growth, Marie had increased 4.6 years. She was now reading above grade level. At the close of the year, all of the class showed substantial growth in reading and language skills, as measured by standardized test scores. This is especially significant for special education teachers as we are held accountable for the children's progress.

During the next summer, I prepared a special class library, known as the "read-aloud collection." Throughout the following year, my class and I enjoyed at least twelve to fifteen novels together. I began with *The Outsiders,* and then read other S. E. Hinton novels during the year: *That Was Then, This Is Now, Tex,* and *Rumble Fish.* Some other all-time favorites are *The Wave,* by Todd Strasser; *Incident at Hawks Hill,* by Allan Eckert; *Killing Mr. Griffin* and *Locked in Time,* by Lois Duncan; *One Fat Summer,* by Robert Lipsyte; *Snow Bound,* by Harry Mazer; and *The War Between the Classes,* by Gloria Miklowitz.

Every year is a marvel to me. Each group of children reacts differently to the novels. Each time I read a novel with a new class, my tone and reading technique vary. There are some constants to the reading program: the love of reading we grow to share and our commitment to read aloud.

References

Adams, Richard. 1975. *Watership Down.* New York: Avon Books.

Atwell, Nancie. 1987. *In the Middle: Writing, Reading, and Learning with Adolescents.* Portsmouth, NH: Boynton/Cook.

Christopher, Matt. 1979. *Ice Magic.* Boston: Little, Brown and Company.

Duncan, Lois. 1978. *Killing Mr. Griffin.* New York: Dell.

———.1985. *Locked in Time.* New York: Dell.

Eckert, Allan W. 1987. *Incident at Hawk's Hill.* New York: Bantam.

Hinton, S. E. 1971. *That Was Then, This Is Now.* New York: Dell.

———. 1975. *Rumble Fish.* New York: Dell.

———. 1979. *Tex.* New York: Dell.

———. 1982. *The Outsiders.* New York: Dell.

Lipsyte, Robert. 1977. *One Fat Summer*. New York: Bantam Books.

Mazer, Harry. 1973. *Snowbound*. New York: Dell.

Miklowitz, Gloria D. 1985. *The War Between The Classes*. New York: Dell.

Pfeffer, Susan Beth. 1980. *About David*. New York: Dell.

Strasser, Todd. 1981. *The Wave*. New York: Dell.

Trelease, Jim. 1985. *The Read-Aloud Handbook*. New York: Penguin.

5. Do You Teach Skills?

Michael Quinn

Since 1983, the regular classroom teachers at Stratham Memorial School have been using a process approach to teaching writing (Graves 1983). The effect on the students' writing was so dramatic that in 1986, teachers began to explore and develop similar approaches to the teaching of reading (Hansen 1987).

By 1987, every classroom teacher was using a process approach to reading and writing. Although classrooms varied in style, important elements were consistent throughout the school (Wansart 1990).

1. A daily quiet time for each child to read and write.
2. Students allowed to choose their writing topics and reading books.
3. Daily sharing of reading or writing in small and large groups.
4. Heterogeneous grouping for instruction.
5. Encouragement of peer interaction to solve problems in reading and writing.

As Stratham's regular classroom teachers adopted these changes, I became aware of a contradiction between these new attitudes toward children and the existing resource room model for special education. While regular classroom instruction grew more individualized and the positive effects of peer teaching were more heavily emphasized in order to meet the needs of students with varied abilities, students with learning disabilities were removed from the classroom to receive individualized instruction in the resource room (Herdecker, Quinn, Wessells, and Wansart 1989).

As a resource room teacher, it was easy for me to see the negative effects of a pull-out model. I wanted my students to read and write daily, to make choices about their reading and writing, and to collaborate on academic problems. Despite my best efforts, this was not happening for my students in the resource room. I believe they avoided reading and writing because of low self-esteem and feelings of incompetence.

In the teachers' room I would hear teachers talk about students who read and wrote during free times and at home, students who read several books at once and had several ideas for stories, students who spoke of the books and stories with understandings beyond what the teachers had ever expected. Many of these students had reading and writing levels that were similar to my students with learning disabilities. These were the positive role models that my students needed.

I began to work with Nancy Herdecker and Mary Ann Wessells, two classroom teachers, and William Wansart, a professor from the University of New Hampshire, to develop a model to deliver special education services in the regular classroom. This model provided students with learning disabilities the support necessary to learn and be successful in process-oriented classrooms (Wansart 1990).

Students with learning disabilities were able to benefit from this setting and were able to change how they viewed learning and how they viewed themselves as learners (Wansart 1989).

Integrating the two classrooms

Teacher changes.   One of many questions that arose during this transition was how to teach skills and strategies to students with learning disabilities in the absence of workbooks and basals. It was clear that the techniques I used with the children would have to be consistent with the approaches used by the classroom teachers. If I failed to do this, I would encourage the false dichotomy of special and regular education, the students would get confusing messages about their reading and writing, and the classroom teachers would be less comfortable interacting with students with learning disabilities. If I asked some students to work on flash cards, word games, or other types of drills while the other children were engaged in reading and writing, then I would be creating a resource room within the regular classroom.

Along with being consistent, the techniques had to teach skills while encouraging the child to read and write more frequently. The children in process classrooms often make choices about which stories to read and write and how challenging they should be. If I could not teach skills in a supportive and encouraging way, I would reinforce the childrens' negative attitudes toward reading and writing. They would be hesitant to make challenging choices as readers and writers; they might even reduce the amount of time they spent reading and writing.

Student changes.   While I worked on changing my teaching techniques, the students with learning disabilities were undergoing their own changes. They began to feel a part of the classroom community; their attitudes towards reading and writing improved; and they began to write and read more frequently. These students were making good choices about their reading and writing. They were not dependent or passive. It was common to hear that students were reading and writing at home and during free times.

With this increase in reading and writing, it became easier to determine exactly what the child knew and what the child's needs were. It became clear that the students' work would not only show if they knew a strategy or skill but it could more accurately show their level of understanding.

Teaching skills and strategies in process classrooms

In order to plan lessons that would build on the knowledge that students had, I categorized their use of skills into five levels:

1. *Mastery*—the student uses a skill consistently in both reading and writing.

2. *Inconsistent use*—the student uses a skill inconsistently in reading and/or writing.

3. *Specific use*—the student is able to use a skill correctly in some situations but is unaware of other uses for the skill.

4. *Overgeneralized use*—the student uses a skill too frequently or incorrectly.

5. *Not used*—the student shows no evidence of a skill in either reading or writing.

After investigating what each of my students knew about reading and writing, I began to develop teaching techniques that would identify needed skills and strategies and encourage their use without discouraging reading and writing.

Mastery. Mastery, for my purposes, is when a child's use of a strategy or skill is consistently correct in both reading and writing. For example, Lisa is a third-grade child who knows that a question mark is used to show that a question is being asked. She uses them when she writes, and when she reads sentences with question marks, her inflection is accurate.

While Lisa shares a story she has written, I make notes of different aspects of her work; there are spelling errors and grammatical mistakes. When she is finished, we discuss the content of her story and I ask her for some clarification.

There are many elements of her writing that we could work on, but I do not want to ignore Lisa's having mastered the use of question marks. We have the following conversation:

Mike: I've noticed in your reading and writing that you know how to use question marks and you use them correctly all the time.

Lisa: [*Smiles*]

Mike: Do you remember when you were in second grade and you used to forget them when you wrote?

Lisa: Yes, but I don't anymore.

Mike: That's right, you just keep learning more and more all the time. I'm very impressed. When you have some time would you help John [*a classmate*] edit his story for question marks?

Lisa: All right.

From there we begin to talk about other aspects of her writing.

Although there is no need to encourage her use of question marks, there is a need to give positive feedback on her accomplishment. I want her to feel good about what she has learned and to feel successful. I want her to bring those feelings with her as we work on difficult areas.

Inconsistent use.   While evaluating the reading and writing of my students, I found frequent examples that suggested a student knew a skill but did not use it each time it was needed. Such is the case with Donna, one of my second graders, who knows that sentences should end with a period but does not always remember to use them. Donna wrote a story about Thanksgiving.

After she shares her story with me, I ask her several questions and comment on the content of her story. I notice that she has used periods twice on the first page of her story but nowhere else. Donna has just become comfortable sharing her stories, and I don't want to give her a negative message or to undo all the positive feelings that this conference has brought her by asking her to correct her punctuation.

It is not necessary to teach Donna how to use periods. She simply needs to remember to use them. Asking her to go over and correct might help her to remember to use periods more frequently, or it might show her that I am more concerned about how she writes than what she has to say. She might decide not to share her writing, or worse, not to write at all. A better way to remind her to use periods is described in the conversation that followed our discussion regarding the content of her story.

Mike: Did you notice what you did in your writing?

Donna: What do you mean?

Mike: You did something that makes it much easier for someone to read your story.

Donna: What?

Mike: You used periods here and here to show where your sentences end. That's very important. It helps me be able to read your story and sound just like you. Great job, Donna.

The smile on Donna's face assures me that she will remember why she should use periods and that she will think about them when she writes.

An example of inconsistent use of a skill in reading is provided by a fourth-grade group of readers made up of Gary, a child with learning disabilities, and two of his classmates. We take turns reading from our choice of reading books. Gary, who relies heavily on phonics as a reading strategy, is reading a book on dinosaurs. He is reading for a while when he comes to the word "scientist," which he begins to pronounce "skine" and then says "scientist" and continues reading.

When he's done we talk about what he knows about dinosaurs from this and other books, and the other students join us in the discussion. Finally, I ask him about the word "scientist" and ask him how he read it.

Gary: I sounded it out.

Mike: Yes, I heard you start to sound it out, but then I thought you did something else.

Gary: What?

Mike: Well, you made the sounds that you saw and came up with "skine" because that's how it looks. But you knew that "skine" would not make sense, and I think that you tried to think of a word that sounds like "skine" that would make sense in that sentence. That is a good skill to use as a reader because many times the rules we know don't always work. Does anyone else do that when they come to a word they don't know?

Everyone in the group agreed they did use the skill, and we went on to talk about other reading strategies. I chose not to teach the soft "c" sound at this point because I felt that it was more important to talk about the use of context cues. Even though Gary thought that phonics was his only strategy, he was using both phonics and context. By identifying it and giving him credit for using this important strategy, I hoped to encourage him to combine these two strategies more frequently.

Both Donna and Gary knew the particular strategy but failed to use it in some instance. One way to call attention to their lapse was to ask them to fix it. Instead, I praised them for the times they used the skill. They heard the same message but were given credit for knowing the strategy. They saw me as a source of information but were not made to feel dependent for cues and information.

They were also given this instruction in the context in which I expected them to use the information. I hoped to help them generalize these skills by using various contexts. Because students with learning disabilities seem to have difficulty transferring bits of information presented out of context (Poplin 1988), I avoid reductionistic approaches, such as phonic flash cards.

Specific use. Another frequent scenario is when a child has a piece of information but does not use the information in various settings or generalize the information to solve new problems. This specific use of a skill is often seen in students' writing.

Carl, a fifth-grade student, shares a story with me about a jungle adventure. While he reads the conversation between his two characters, he lets me know that the characters are taking turns talking by changing the tone of his voice to match the character. He doesn't use quotation marks in his writing, but he uses his voice to show that conversation is taking place. Several days earlier, Carl had showed me that he understood quotation marks when he read them in *Johnny Tremain.*

These two pieces of information suggest an ideal opportunity to teach Carl how to use quotation marks. Carl is aware that he needs a device for writing, but doesn't use his knowledge of reading to solve his problem. After questions and comments about his story, our discussion turns to quotation marks.

Mike: I enjoyed the way you read the characters' conversation. I could tell that people were talking. Do you know how you let me know?

Carl: Yeah, I changed my voice.

Mike: That's right. Do you know other ways that you could let a reader know that characters are talking without using your voice?

Carl: I could capitalize the words they said.

Mike: I have seen that. Sometimes when the author wants you to know that a character yelled or was excited, they will capitalize words like "WOW." Take out the book you're reading and let's see if the author uses any other ways.

Carl: [*Before the book is even open*] Quotation marks!

Mike: That's right. Look at how they're used.

We go on to discuss the placement of quotation marks and the use of paragraphs to delineate speakers. Along with learning how to use quotation marks, Carl makes the connection between his reading and his writing. I emphasize this connection frequently, encouraging him to build on what he knows to solve new challenges in his reading and writing

Jessica is a sixth-grade student who is building her knowledge of phonic rules so that she may increase her reading and spelling strategies. Jessica reads a passage to me that she has picked from her latest book. She uses many different strategies when she reads, but misses about ten words. Although she read the word "madly," three of the words she misses contain the suffix "ly." After a conversation about the content and how Jessica feels the book is different from the movie, we turn to skills.

Mike: Jessica, this word you read is an interesting word.

Jessica: Madly?

Mike: Yes, do you notice something interesting about it?

Jessica: [*After some thought*] No.

Mike: It has "ly" at the end of it. "Ly" is a common ending that is sometimes attached to a word to change its meaning. [*Covering the "ly" to expose "mad"*] If you take the "ly" off, most of the time you are left with a complete word and it is easier to read.

Jessica: [*Nods her head to say she understands*]

Mike: Let's see how often this idea works. Let's go through your story and look for words with "ly" in them.

Together we find all the words with the pattern and she breaks them apart and reads them. She has been given the same message ("ly" says a certain sound) as she would have been given through memorizing flash cards. But she has learned that "ly" makes a certain sound and has used that information in the context of her reading. This type of lesson also shows her how frequently she can expect to find this specific phonic pattern, and she may also find some exceptions to the rule. Failing to expose children to this information adds to the difficulty of learning to apply rules to daily reading and writing.

As in Carl's case, Jessica had some knowledge that she couldn't apply. Through instruction, she was given credit for knowing a word and she was shown, in the context of reading, how to use that information to solve other words. This skill helps to break the dependent learning style that is often attributed to students with learning disabilities (Torgensen 1983).

Overgeneralized use.   In reviewing the children's work, I found several examples of a child using a skill or strategy correctly in some instances but relying too heavily on it or using the skill incorrectly at other times. Once again, Jessica provides an example. Jessica is extremely consistent in her use of phonics when she writes. Earlier this year she learned that "ou" made the sound that is heard in the word "out." Her reliance on this information helps her spell many words correctly. However, she is overdependent on this pattern, creating words such as "hou" and "allou."

There are two goals I hoped to accomplish in working with Jessica. First, I hoped to teach her other strategies for improving her spelling, as reliance on phonics for spelling will always be problematic. Second, I hoped to help her refine her understanding of the use of specific letter/sound associations such as "ou" in spelling.

Jessica shares a piece of writing with me. She has used "ou" to spell several words correctly, such as "out" and "found," but has overused it in two words, "hou" and "allou." Again, I start by discussing the content of her story. (It is essential to remember that conveying an idea is the reason that people write. I do not wish to lose that message by focusing most heavily on the mechanics of writing.) After going over her story, I focus on spelling.

Mike: Jessica, you have done a great job of spelling in your story. It is easy to read, and I can tell you worked hard at it.

Jessica: Thanks.

Mike: You spelled a couple of tricky ones. How did you remember to use "ou" to spell "out" and "found"?

Jessica: I just knew it I guess.

Mike: I think that's great. Those words are tricky because there is more than one way to spell that sound you hear. The letters ""ow" will also make that sound too. But "ow" is usually used at the end of a word, not in the middle. Let's go through the book you are reading and look for words with that sound and see how often that rule works.

Going through a few pages of her book we find several words with the "ou"/"ow" sound: around, how, out, about, houses, howl, powers, now, round, encounter, down, plow, and cow. She also points to several words that have "ou" in them but do not have the sound for which we are looking. We agree to return to the use of "ou" at another time. After reviewing the words in her book, we agree to modify the rule that I had suggested.

Jessica: Sometimes "ow" does come in the middle of the word. [*She seems quite pleased with finding the evidence to prove me wrong.*]

Mike: Yes, I guess that isn't quite right, is it? What if I change the rule to this: When that sound comes at the end of the word it is *usually* spelled with "ow."

Jessica agrees with this new rule, and we go on to test its accuracy. She learns what she might have learned if she had corrected her misspellings, but she learns it in a nonthreatening way. She also learns that she can challenge the strategies and rules she has developed or been taught and refine their use, much like a toddler develops his or her understanding of spoken language.

A student who I worked with two years ago was similar to Gary in his approach to reading. Chris relied entirely on phonics and read letter by letter. He amazed me by reading words like "was" and "the" as if he were sounding them out, when of course he could not. Even though he recognized common words like these, his overgeneralized use of phonics was causing him to read in a choppy manner.

Mike: Chris, you are doing a good job of reading. You are working very hard to get each word. Can you tell me how you got this word, "was"?

Chris: I sounded it out.

Mike: Do you know that there are some other ways to recognize words when you are reading? I am going to read from your book [*Where the Wild Things Are*], and I won't let you see the words. I think that you will be able to read some of the words anyway.

Chris: [*Expresses disbelief*]

Mike: " 'Now stop!' Max _____ . . . "

Chris: Said?

Mike: Right! "And Max the king of all wild _____ was lonely. . . . "

Chris: Things!

Mike: How did you know that?

Chris: I don't know.

Mike: I think that you knew those words because you understand how books are written and you've sounded out the word "thing" in the beginning of this story. Sometimes it's easier to think about what word would make sense than it is to sound every word out.

This one discussion didn't change Chris's reading overnight, but we frequently had variations of this discussion as I tried to move him into using other word recognition strategies. Gradually, Chris began to trust his contextual knowledge, and his reading became more fluent.

Not used.   Sometimes, though not as often as I originally thought, I am not able to teach a skill using some information that the child has shown me. In those cases, I use my own writing or another student's writing to demonstrate. This lesson is an example of teaching a child a skill that they have not used at all.

In a second-grade classroom, all the children are seated around Jill as she shares her latest piece of writing. Her story is well received by the class, and they make positive comments and ask her a few questions. One of the techniques that Jill displayed in her writing was the use of dialogue and narrative to tell her story. It is a strategy that Sarah, a student in the group, has not yet attempted.

I raise my hand to make a comment to Jill.

Jill: Mr. Quinn?

Mike: Jill, I really like the way you tell your story and also tell what people say. I think that sometimes it makes the story more interesting. Do you usually do that in your writing?

Jill: Sometimes it makes the story more real.

In this case, Jill stands as a model for Sarah. Without being told that she should use more dialogue and that without the technique her writing is not interesting, she is nevertheless exposed to this strategy. Because of my comment and the class's positive response to Jill's story, Sarah learns what the audience (her teachers and classmates) appreciate in writing. Consequently, Sarah's next piece included a small amount of dialogue.

David is another example of a child learning a new skill from a role model. I am reading with two third-grade children: David, who is identified as having a learning disability, and Joey, who is not. Joey is reading while David and I listen. Joey's reading is marked with great intonation, a skill to which David pays little attention. When Joey is finished, I make several comments and specifically mention his intonation. David does the same and also remarks on the excitement in Joey's voice. While David reads, he pays attention to his voice and the storyline. Though his book is easier to read and his intonation not as strong as Joey's, David is praised for the quality of his reading by his classmate and by me.

David was able to hear Joey's intonation and, partially because of the praise Joey received, he chose to imitate it. In essence, David does something that is essential to meaningful and lifelong learning; he set a goal for himself and began working on it. By using a peer to model and praising him for it, I am able to expose David to new skills and strategies in a positive way.

Redefining needs

In my years as a teacher of children with learning disabilities, I have focused primarily on the "special needs" of my students, and I have been outraged when schools or educators would ignore those special needs. Regretfully, I have been equally at fault for my students' continued frustrations because I have ignored their more "normal needs," those needs that I accept in regular classroom students and in myself. These needs include:

1. The need to feel confident and competent as learners.

2. The need to learn skills so they can express themselves or understand others more clearly, not because the teacher or the curriculum mandates it.

3. The need to feel accepted and respected in a community of learners where learning is safe and nonthreatening.

If these needs are not met, the desire to read and write may collapse under the pressure of self-doubt and feelings of incompetence.

I use the techniques described here in order to teach skills and strategies to students with learning disabilities in the context of a regular classroom that uses a process approach to reading and writing. They allow me to teach children in a manner that is complimentary and consistent with the techniques used by the regular classroom teachers. They can be used with individual children or mixed groups of children with learning disabilities and their nonhandicapped peers.

These approaches encourage children to read and write more frequently because they are not overwhelmed by all that they need to learn. Instead, the emphasis is on what they are able to do. Encouraging children to expand their knowledge to develop new skills empowers them to take control of their learning.

References

Graves, Donald H. 1983. *Writing: Teachers and Children at Work.* Portsmouth, NH: Heineman.

Hansen, Jane. 1987. *When Writers Read.* Portsmouth, NH: Heinemann.

Herdecker, N., M. Quinn, M. Wessells, and W. Wansart. 1989. "Students with Learning Disabilities in Process Classrooms." Paper presented at the 11th International Conference on Learning Disabilities, Denver, Colorado.

Poplin, Mary S. 1988. "The Reductionistic Fallacy in Learning Disabilities: Replicating the Past by Reducing the Present." *Journal of Learning Disabilities* 21 (August/ September): 389–400.

Torgensen, J. K. 1983. "The Learning Disabled Child as an Inactive Learner: Educational Implications." *Topics in Learning Disabilities* 2: 45–52.

Sendak, Maurice, 1963. *Where the Wild Things Are.* New York: Harper and Row.

Wansart, William L. 1989. "The Student with Learning Disabilities in a Writing Process Classroom: A Case Study." *Journal of Reading, Writing, and Learning Disabilities* 4: 311–319.

———. 1990. "The Classroom Is the Resource: Mainstreaming Students with Learning Disabilities at Stratham Memorial School." *Intervention* 26(1): 48–51.

6. Pull Out or Put In?

Karen Robinson

An ongoing debate revolves around whether it is better to pull a child out of class or put an additional instructor in the classroom to help children who appear to need extra instruction in reading and writing. What I have learned after fifteen years of teaching in a variety of settings, including eight as a Chapter 1 teacher in both pull-out and put-in programs, is that instruction is best offered in a classroom environment that promotes both literacy and self-esteem. Learning successfully in school depends, I believe, on the degree to which students are encouraged to follow their interests and make choices about how their chosen texts, both written and read, fit into the context of their social and academic situation.

The positive academic effects of social interaction in a classroom are just beginning to be recognized, whereas the stigmatizing effects of ability grouping and labeling are well documented (Purkey 1984). Many parents envision their child moving along an academic assembly line from grade to grade. When extra help is suggested, parents wonder whether their child is a "lemon" on the line.

When I talked to Mary's mother at the start of her daughter's second-grade year, she worried that Mary was "not smart" and would feel "singled out" by having Chapter 1 instruction. This common attitude creates a dilemma for me as a Chapter 1 teacher because my first goal for any student is to promote self-esteem. In my dual role as principal and half-time Chapter 1 teacher in a small, rural elementary school, I see not only parents who are anxious, but also others in the community who are bitter. These adults feel that receiving special services kept them from achieving their potential. Further, educational research shows that specialists continue to "help" the same students year after year, almost automatically tracking them into vocational courses at the high school level. "When they put me in the bonehead class," one student wrote, "I wanted to walk out the door and never come back" (Purkey 1984,13).

Many children in Chapter 1 programs have difficulty organizing themselves to follow through with the kinds of reading and writing tasks required in school. Some come from disorganized and unsupportive home environments. Chapter 1 students, like most children, are eager and want to learn. They tend to frustrate easily, however. They soon see themselves as not doing well and, confirming their parents fears, are quick to call themselves "stupid." Sometimes, parents of Chapter 1 students can't read or were "slow learners" themselves in school.

Pull-out programs

The problem with pull-out for the classroom teacher is orchestration of programs and schedules so that children involved do not miss regular instruction or special subjects such as art and physical education. Students receiving extra help should not be penalized later by having to make up assignments missed in class. Many teachers find these scheduling logistics to be more disruptive than helpful. When a student asks "Can I go back early so I can get my math done before recess?" the child has obviously received a message: Get back in time to do the missed math or stay in at recess and do it.

Some classroom teachers believe that Chapter 1 students must complete all classroom assignments, as well as receive extra help. Some students also feel that they should do classroom assignments in order to fit in and belong to the class. Often the purpose of the assignment as a learning opportunity is not acknowledged. Rather, it is something to be completed, handed in, and checked off. The pressure to complete such assignments is unfair and unnecessary.

I believe that pull-out programs are less problematic in speech, guidance, and special education areas where the pull-out teacher plans and teaches the entire curriculum, but they are not necessarily helpful:

There is no compelling body of evidence that segregated special education programs have significant benefits for students. On the contrary, there is substantial and growing evidence that goes in the opposite direction. In a sense, regular and special education teachers have colluded to relieve regular teachers of responsibilities for teaching children functioning at the bottom of their class. (Gartner and Lipsky 1987, 61)

Pull-out programs are particularly problematic for Chapter 1 and special education teachers who support students. In my view, it is reasonable to ask what a specialist can do for a child that a classroom teacher cannot. The corollary question then becomes: Who needs what kind of help from the specialist?

The major difficulty for the specialist is planning and pacing for pull-out student instruction with the classroom teacher. Despite everyone's best intentions, specialized instruction often takes place in a vacuum, with the specialist doing program "A" while the classroom teacher continues program "B." For example, if the Chapter 1 teacher is helping a third-grade child develop reading strategies and the child returns to the classroom to struggle with complex directions and content reading material written at or beyond the child's grade level, the child might rightly feel a sense of failure.

Even when the same skill is supposedly called for by both specialist and classroom teacher, the program material may cause a roadblock. Here is a typical example of the kind of confusion that can reign. Bonnie "failed" a commercially designed worksheet on alphabetical order. When I gave her word cards to put in piles, she quickly and correctly alphabetized them after estimating in which half of the dictionary each would be located. The worksheet had required her to read multiple directions and place her choices in numerical order. Bonnie did not have difficulty with alphabetical order. She could not correlate numerical and alphabetical order, a different and more complicated skill.

Sometimes I think we stack the deck against children who are having trouble in school. They are the children who can least afford to miss regular instruction and are likely to have the most difficulty with transitions. Yet we routinely ask a child to leave the room daily for, say, Chapter 1 reading and special education math, twice weekly for guidance, and once a week for speech. We also need to remember when we evaluate children at the lower end of the bell curve that they have learned early to expect failure when compared to others in their grade. Children who do not expect to do well generally don't. When questionable test results are used to indicate a child's progress, or lack of it, the cycle of failure renews itself. From the children's point of view it seems that no matter how much they learn they will always be behind. I think it is unfortunate that, outside of athletics, students are seldom offered goal-referenced measures of success that reflect individual improvement or gains over time.

Is it better to have the specialist in the room? I believe it is for several reasons. First, as a specialist, I become part of the child's learning environment, which means there is no transition to be made and nothing for the child to make up. Secondly, the teacher and specialist can shift gears together to meet student needs on the spot. Finally, the opportunity to connect children, both in and out of the program, is a way to let them know that it's okay to get help and, especially, it's okay to help each other.

Specialists can provide stimulation and variety in the classroom by using new materials and demonstrating alternative strategies. Switching roles with classroom teachers is a very productive way to share professional knowledge and model different teaching styles. This can occur when the specialist teaches or manages the whole class, allowing the classroom teacher to work with individual students for a while.

There are times when I pull out, but only as needed. I take out the third graders to practice their months—"Thirty days hath September. . . "—and my second graders for choral reading of a poem. I may work with a student on word processing during writing time. Because a specialist can move, I can produce dramatic events or special projects, generate opportunites for cross-grade sharing, and provide follow-up visits to the library for a student to get a book or look up and collect information. The teacher sets the stage in the classroom and I pick up from there. We feel good when our teacher intuitions get in synch, like two unrelated heart muscle cells placed side by side that miraculously begin to pulse together, even though they are from two different hearts.

Fitting into first grade

Children thrive in the emerging literacy environment in Adrianne Gallant's first grade at my school. Last year she established a classroom that fits this description:

> The literate environment of this classroom is based on sound principles of child development and language learning. In this environment whole language and a variety of learning experiences, oral and written, provide the functional context for reading and writing development. This necessarily requires that language not be segmented into abstract skills nor separated from sociolinguistic context. Evaluation is formative, descriptive, qualitative, and longitudinal, and involves samples of students' work. (Wortman and Haussler 1989, 46)

Children in Mrs. Gallant's classroom freely express their enthusiasm for literacy; many are writing their way into reading. They progress through representational writing and use of invented spelling toward recognition and use of standard spelling as they focus on meaning. For the first half of the year I listened to children read and share their beginning writing during learning-center time. All of the children in Mrs. Gallant's classroom believe themselves to be readers and writers because that is what they do every day. They evaluate their achievement in terms of how far they see themselves progressing over time. At midyear we selected a few children who had not yet formally begun to read for me to work with in the classroom.

John and Jeremy have been slow to want to read and write. They would rather draw and talk. Jeremy made a big poster of his "stomper" and dictated a sentence to me. Meanwhile, Mrs. Gallant provided word boxes for the boys and a few other students. Every day a new word of their choosing is added to the box. Jeremy picked the word "fire" from his poster. Later, Jeremy and John made a big book about wheels together. After each poster they drew, I helped them write their ideas, transcribed the spelling, and they copied it over on their posters. It made quite a book. They can read it to the class. They are readers and writers in their own context. They do not feel stupid. For these students, writing and reading are not separated; author and audience together make print meaningful. "Both the reader and the writer must identify appropriate background information, create a text, make inferences, plan, search for unity, self-correct, and so on" (Harste, Woodward, and Burke 1984, 134). A book read together leads to an idea that evolves around a shared interest among friends, and leads again to new books written by friends for friends. A pull-out program does not facilitate this cycle of success.

Children's choices in second grade

Second-grade teacher Vicki Meisner structures her classroom environment so that when I come for reading, all the children are doing choice reading and writing. This allows me to engage Chapter 1 students individually and in pairs. Here are some vignettes.

One bright October day Rita wrote a book about rainbows that contained questions for her readers. We discussed who might answer them and she said, "My friends." I gave her a clipboard, and she read her book to each classmate, in turn, and wrote their responses, interview style, on her clipboard. Two responses were the same. Rita exercised her author's prerogative and asked if one of the girls could word hers differently. Erin gladly complied by changing "It is pretty" to "It is pretty in the air." Rita could control her text and get the help she asked for from her teacher and her friends.

Rita does not yet know she is "behind" according to standardized test measures. She sees herself and the people around her as authors and readers because she can communicate freely with them in print. By pulling Rita out of the room, I could not have taken advantage of the literacy environment that connects Rita with her friends and with her purposes for reading and writing. Rita the author needs her audience; Rita the reader needs to exchange ideas with classmates. Her choices remain unlimited in the classroom.

When children choose books, they feel free to explore the text actively rather than wait for teacher-selected vocabulary. Since the emphasis is on meaning, children find opportunities to explore the symbols used to convey meaning. Erin finds logical relationships between reading and spelling in her text. She notices that words are not necessarily pronounced the way they are spelled. We encountered the word "laughed." We talked about the many pronunciations of "gh" words as she pointed to "bought." She examined each page of her book to find other examples. Two other students nearby listened to our conversation and pointed out some "gh" words in their books. I followed Erin's lead so she could learn what was important to her.

Jon and Randy wanted to read a story to me about a tattletale. I asked them to read it to themselves first, and as they did, they asked me about some of the words. We looked at "tough," "laughed," "throughout," and "tongue." Since they weren't fluent reading this book aloud, I read the story to them. We sat together under a table, one small group among other pairs and threes huddled in nooks and corners around the carpeted room. We talked about tattletales and why little brothers and sisters tattle so much. Randy decided it was because they were trying to get even with their older siblings who always got everything. Jon and I were older siblings. We agreed. We were readers together, using the author's scenario to share our feelings and thoughts. They did not have to read all the print symbols in the story to be successful readers. They were successful readers because they used the author's meaning to make their own meaning. They will read the symbols, in time, because they want to.

Erin, Rita, Bonnie, and I took parts in a play, "The Frog and the Dragon," which we rehearsed several times and presented to the class. Another group, made up of some of the same people, performance-read a play. Later in the week, several others wrote and read their plays. Since one good idea leads to another, short and humorous plays generated a classroom fad for a couple of weeks. I helped several groups practice and put on plays, whether they were all Chapter 1 students or not. These opportunities occur only in the classroom.

Terry read about a nodding sunflower. He wanted to know why it didn't stay up with nails. He could understand the tape failing, but nails? I had to leave so I asked Kyle to help him figure out why the nails didn't hold the sunflower up. Kyle, like Terry, is highly inquisitive about how things work. As I left, they were gesturing animatedly and proposing theories as they engaged in finding the revealing descriptive paragraph. I left. The learning continued.

Does it matter that Terry receives Chapter 1 services and Kyle is designated "gifted and talented"? These two can share at a comparable intellectual level, meeting both their needs at once: Kyle's need to be stimulated by real problems and Terry's need to understand what he reads.

Mrs. Gallant and Mrs. Meisner both keep daily records of reading and writing conferences with their students. When I come in, I have my own sheet to complete as I conference with students. At the end of the week, I copy it and give it to the classroom teacher with my comments. We have a brief conference to check on each child, making rough plans for the following week. We share information equally as co-teachers, and the children benefit from the double attention.

Synergy in third grade

The following thirty minutes in a third-grade writing group represents what I believe is an example of my Chapter 1 involvement. All our activities were related back to the classroom teacher's plans, with no wasted time or energy. Even though this was writing, the revision and sharing required reading and critical thinking, for we understand the inseparability of reading and writing. But it was more than good teacher coordination and more than a well-planned lesson. It was a magical time for us.

Ben and Jim found they had different ideas about the safety of three- and four-wheelers as Jim read his text. Their discussion allowed Jim to put more of his specific knowledge into his paper. He added, "But four-wheelers and three-wheelers are dangerous. When you ride your four-wheeler and do wheelies, you flip a lot of times. My Uncle John does pop-up wheelies with his four wheeler." I volunteered the title "All Wheelers" (which he loved) because he was talking about more than one kind of vehicle. Mike then read his story about two robbers to us and responded to our plea that he make an addition so as not to leave us "hanging" at the end. Ben read us his jet story, which we duly appreciated. Imbued with their power as writers, Ben and Mike drafted a good-bye card to their music teacher while I continued working with Jim. They proudly read it to us and put it on the computer. We all felt so good about ourselves and each other. I find that when students are in control of their own learning, they tune in. When I tune in to their learning, I can teach more effectively. "By allowing children to show us when instruction will be most effective, less time is wasted presenting material to a group at a time when it might be inappropriate or unimportant for particular children" (Cadieux 1988, 79).

What made this class special was that as soon as I entered the room, I knew they were excited about their writing; not only Mike, Ben, and Jim, but others, too. They were sharing with each other and working on their stories in small writing groups. I knew our immediate goal was revision with an eye to publishing. I knew I was in the midst of a "moment of passion" in learning (Ely and

Anzul 1989). I believe these special moments between teachers and children are what keep us all going. The following serendipity occurred during a group reading conference in third grade.

When we discussed a mystery Ben had read, several students became excited about the genre. Alec shared the book he was reading and asked if he could show us a "spooky" book. Alec was so excited to read the newly discovered mystery, I asked him to go off with Ben so they could read it together. Mike wanted to go. So he went, too. Danny and Jim wanted to share their books with me. I asked Jim to read his first chapter silently before sharing, since he hadn't had a chance to read it to himself yet. While he read quietly on the floor next to me, Danny shared his book with me. We talked about book selection. Danny noticed that the description on the back was harder to read than the book. Then, Abby read the first paragraph of her series book to me as others were getting ready for lunch. She said it was the longest book she'd ever tried and wanted to give it a go. Some of us were late for lunch, but nobody minded.

Kids are always tuning in to each other about what is good to read. Many common interests are explored and projects developed from this kind of shared reading. Children know the resources of their classroom and use them. This "process-based" instruction is a far cry from the constricted round-robin reading groups of my youth. According to Jane Hansen, a former Chapter 1 teacher herself: "Everyone rightfully expects us to teach comprehension, vocabulary, and skills, but we must have the right to teach them the way we think is best. We can teach our students to choose their books and respond to those choices. We, in turn, respond to what they know, and when we sense a need, we teach something new. We have the authority to point out constantly to our students what they know rather than what they don't know" (Hansen 1987, 183).

Children learn all the time. As a teacher I want to celebrate the learning, to keep it going, to increase the magic moments. I want to be an integral part of a humanitarian literacy-learning environment that defies the people-as-product-oriented factory model. In another time, a great teacher described how she responded to her very special student, creating the most well-known magic moment in educational history. Anne Sullivan wrote in her diary: "I find it much easier to teach [Helen Keller] things at odd moments than at set times" (Keller 1965, 187). When she led Helen to the famous water pump, it was an inspiration of the moment. She followed her well-honed teacher instincts. I believe we need to encourage each other to apply our teacher instincts more often. This happens for me when I am in classrooms.

References

Cadieux, Sharron. 1988. "Letting Children Lead the Way." In *Understanding Writing*, edited by Thomas Newkirk and Nancie Atwell. Portsmouth, NH: Heinemann.

Ely, Margot, and Margaret Anzul. 1989. "Moments of Passion: On Looking Out of the Corner of One's Eye." *Language Arts* 66 (November): 746–747.

Gartner, Alan, and Dorothy K. Lipsky. 1987. "Beyond Special Education Toward a Quality System for All Students." *Harvard Educational Review* 57(4): 61.

Hansen, Jane. 1987. *When Writers Read.* Portsmouth, NH: Heinemann.

Harste, Jerome, Virginia Woodward, and Carolyn Burke. 1984. *Language Stories and Literacy Lessons.* Portsmouth, NH: Heinemann.

Keller, Helen. 1965. *The Story of My Life.* New York: Airmont.

Purkey, William. 1984. *Inviting School Success.* Belmont, CA: Wadsworth.

Wortman, Robert, and Myna Matlin Haussler. 1989. "Evaluation in a Classroom Environment Designed for Whole Language." In *The Whole Language Evaluation Book,* edited by Kenneth S. Goodman, Yetta M. Goodman, and Wendy J. Hood. Portsmouth, NH: Heinemann.

II. Portraits of Readers and Writers

7. Growing as a Writer: L. D. and All

Susan Stires

When Andrea first answered my question "Are you a writer?" at the start of our school writing project, she said yes. To the follow-up question "How did you learn to write?" she replied that she had learned cursive writing in the second grade. Although I knew that Andrea was defining writing in its most basic form—handwriting (Moffett 1981)—I also knew that it was a starting point from which our work could proceed. I had chosen Andrea, a fifth grader, as my case study because of my need to understand her problems as a language user and to learn how to help her improve her brief, incoherent prose.

During her first three years in school, Andrea had received language therapy. In third grade she was evaluated by the school psychologist because of her increasing difficulties in the classroom. He found that she had major problems in sequencing, memory, and abstract reasoning, and she was enrolled in the resource room as a learning disabled student. In fourth grade she was dismissed from language therapy, but her resource room program was to include language development. During that year—my first as a resource room teacher—I searched for effective ways to help Andrea improve her language, writing, and reading comprehension, but with little gain. I felt that I did not have the necessary theoretical background in language and writing development. Fortunately, Nancie Atwell had initiated and developed a school-wide writing project that same year, which began the following summer. During the first series of training sessions, I learned what writing is and how it can be taught most effectively. In the fall, I began teaching writing and conducting research. As a teacher-researcher in the resource room, I examined the specific nature of my students' writing disabilities, while focusing on Andrea as my case study.

Combining research techniques with process/conference approaches gave me insights into Andrea's writing disability. By being involved with her process as she wrote and by looking closely at everything she did, I found that she needed collaboration during the stage of generating ideas, often called rehearsal (Graves 1982), and during revision. I also needed to be available at other stages of the process—drafting, editing, and rewriting—but to a lesser extent.

Content conferences: generating ideas

Andrea had few effective rehearsal strategies during the first year of the writing project and our study. She used techniques that her classroom teacher or I taught (brainstorming, time lines, memory chains, poetry forms, and researching content-area subjects), since she had writing instruction in both settings. She also copied the topic choices and other ideas of her classmates, or drafted without rehearsal. Almost without exception, Andrea needed to go back to rehearsal in order to revise her pieces. Certainly, this move is one utilized by many writers, but Andrea had to be shown that this was necessary because she had no notion that her drafts were incomplete and disorganized. She was unable to detect that what she had written was meaningless to her reader. And she was unable to change her writing without response.

When I looked back over the patterns that developed during our first year of writing, I realized that, although I had been focusing my instruction on revision, I had been constantly demonstrating ways for Andrea to go back to rehearsal: making lists, taking notes, sketching, and most especially, talking. I discovered the powerful effect of talk when Andrea kept a journal of her experiences during an environmental study week in the spring. After participating in a morning of firsthand outdoor activities, Andrea took part in classroom discussions that were followed by journal writing. The pages of her journal were filled with clear, first-draft prose.

Another time that Andrea wrote a meaningful first draft was when she wrote to a favorite author, Judy Blume, in March of her fifth-grade year. This was her second letter to Judy Blume; she had written before, in the fall, when a number of her fifth-grade classmates had written to favorite authors, but no return letter came. In March, Andrea's resource room friend, a sixth grader, wrote to Judy Blume and received a reply. This prompted Andrea to write again. Before she drafted, Andrea took out the final copy of her first letter to Judy Blume from her cumulative folder and reread it. It helped her to generate ideas for her second letter. The first draft of her first letter (Figure 7–1) was partially copied from her classmates' letters. The first draft of her second letter (Figure 7–2), although it has the same lead sentence, is more appropriate in content and organization.

During the second year of the writing project and our study, when Andrea was in sixth grade, I focused on helping her become more independent and successful during the early stages of writing. I continued to demonstrate techniques for topic selection and rehearsal, and I provided models—myself and other students—to demonstrate ways for generating ideas. I also did a lot more talking with Andrea, either in one-to-one conferences or in small groups, prior to drafting. The purpose of this talk about content was to allow Andrea to recreate the essence and sequence of an experience. Further, I talked with Andrea about the ways that she could generate ideas. The purpose of this talk about process helped her remember the many choices that she had, and it helped produce an awareness of the importance of the stages prior to drafting. Finally, I tried to be consistent about pointing out where and how her rehearsal had been effective. As time went by, she was able to tell me where she had been effective.

Figure 7–1

Andrea's first Judy Blume letter.

Back narrows Rd
boothbay me 1#
04557

September 22, 198_

Dear Judy Blume;

I like (your books:). especlly igges - house.
how many books do you write. iv Read
five ob your books I like yous books alot.
iv Read other books too. here is some
other books. winnie the pooh and happy
hollisters enclapeda brown no place
to hide in other words Charolete web.

siserely yours

Figure 7–2

Andrea's second Judy Blume letter.

draft

Ms. Judy Blume
c/o Dell Publishing Co.
New york, New york 10017

March 23
Back narrows Rd.
Boothbay, Maine 04537
March 23, 198_

← Dear Judy Blume,

I like your books a lot cspecially Eggies House.
I wrote a letter last fall. Did you get it? I hope you did,
but I haven't heard from you. Maybe you didnt get it.
I've read Freckle Juice, which is a good story.   I've read:-
← Tales of the Forth Grade Nothing, Shiela the Great, and Blubber.
← I've enjoyed them all.
     . I'd like a pamphlet about you? Could you send
. one? to me?

Sincerly yours,

Content conferences: revision

When I began teaching revision to Andrea during the first year of the writing project and our study, I concentrated on the organization of her pieces. I asked her questions like: Does this belong with this? Where would this go best? You were talking about this here and then again down here. Should these ideas go together?

Figure 7–3

Examples of Andrea's early drafts.

Nov. 10·11

Tittle   The Dog I used to have.   Draft !

I had a dog named peppi. He was a dachund he was a very nice dog but some times he barks . allso he botherd the nebros so we sold him because he barks alot. allso he was brown. he had a dog house that he liked very muich. Somtimes I let him in the house to have his food and milk he liked them to he liked all kinds of dog food . now I have a cat.

Draft 2 #

The dog I used to have.
I had a dog named Peppi. He was a Dachund. He was very nice but sometimes he barked. allso he bothered the neibors. cowe sold him because he barks alot. also he was brown. He had a dog house that he liked way much. Sometimes I let him him in the house to have his food. and milk. He liked all kinds of dog food.
Now I have a cat.

At first, Andrea merely recopied drafts (see Figure 7–3) with minor revisions coming only after a conference. However, with time, Andrea became increasingly better at correcting organizational problems. She learned to circle sentences, draw arrows, number different parts, underline different parts in different colors, cut apart a draft and tape it back together, or revise by writing different parts on different sheets of paper. By the beginning of her second year of writing, she could make any revisions on her own (see Figure 7–4).

Andrea also learned to add to her writing to make it complete, and, in the process, she began to recognize where her ideas were incompletely stated. She learned to add appropriate information and details and to delete irrelevant information and details in order to clarify her writing. The questions I asked Andrea were highly dependent on the content, questions such as:

Figure 7–4

An example from Andrea's second year of writing.

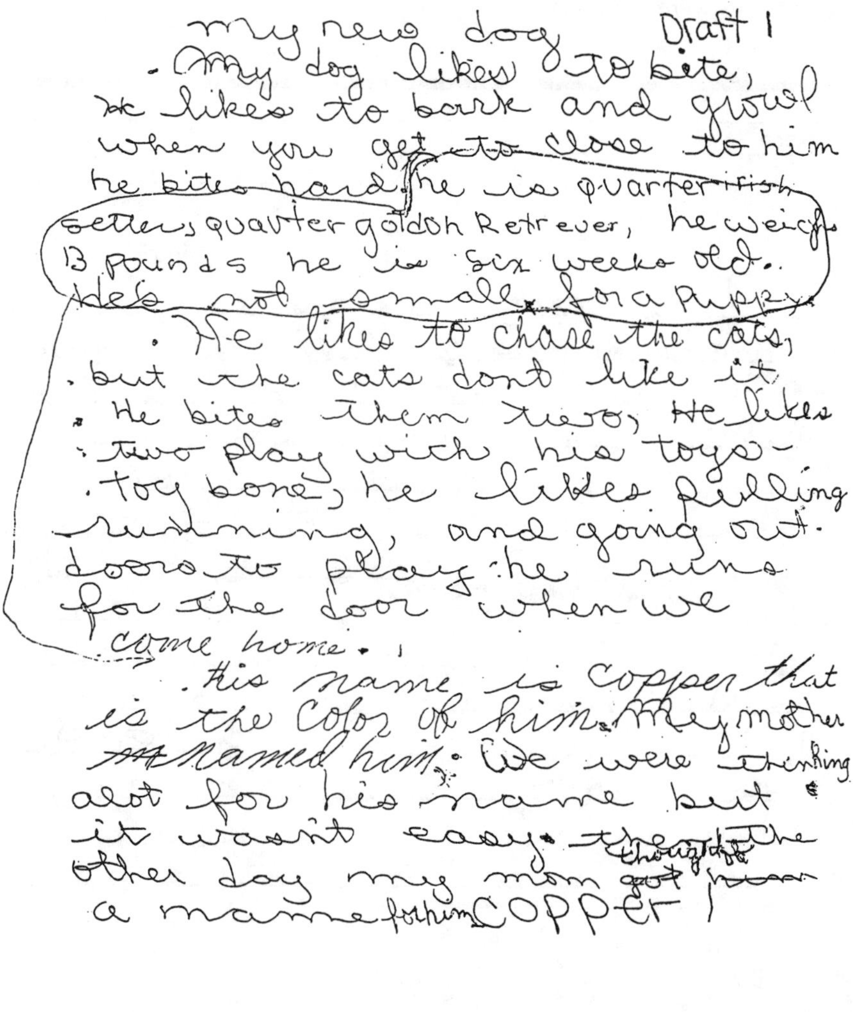
my new dog Draft 1
. My dog likes to bite,
he likes to bark and growl
when you get ~~to close~~ to him
he ~~bites~~ hard. he is quarter ~~Irish~~
setter, quarter goldon Retrever, he weighs
13 pounds he is six weeks old.
~~He's not small for a puppy.~~
. He likes to chase the cats,
. but the cats dont like it.
. He bites them two, He likes
. two play with his toys-
. toy bone, he likes pulling
running, and going out-
doors to play: he runs
for the door when we
come home.
. his name is Copper that
is the Color of him. My mother
named him. We were thinking
alot for his name but
it wasn't easy. ~~the~~ The
other day my mom thought of ~~a~~
a name for him COPPER!

I heard you say—(Paraphrase.)

Did you mean———?

Is there anything else that you know about———?

Is there anything else that happened when———?

Was anyone else with you?

Is this important to your story?

Who is "we"?

Although the questions are not unlike the ones that could be asked of any student, I was careful in how I asked them of Andrea because of her needs as a writer and language user. First of all, I had to be highly consistent about my responses; I had to recognize which questions were the essential ones, the ones that helped her accomplish her purposes without overloading her; I had to give her time and opportunities to talk about what she thought; and I had to give her choices, and not impose my choices by giving direction. In the piece about the day she got her dog, written in the spring of her sixth-grade year, Andrea demonstrated her ability to exclude unimportant details (in draft one, Figure 7–5) and include more related information (in draft two, Figure 7–6). Both of the revisions were self-initiated.

Figure 7–5

Draft one of Andrea's dog piece.

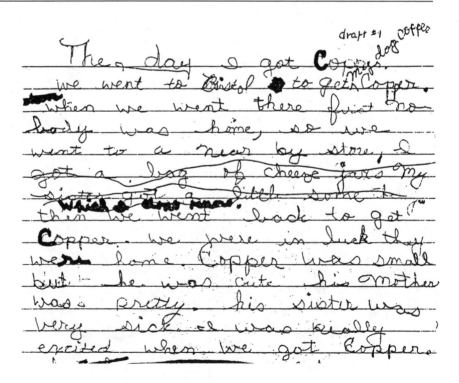

It was important for Andrea to develop ways of putting herself in her writing rather than recording events as an outsider. However, she needed help with how to include her thoughts, feelings, ideas, and opinions in her writing. I asked, in oral and written forms, questions such as the following:

How did you feel when————?

Can you remember what you were thinking about when————?

How do you feel about this now?

What made this special to you?

Figure 7–6

Draft two of Andrea's dog piece.

The Day I got Copper
We went to Bristol to get my dog
copper. When we went there, first nobody
was home, so we went to a nearby store and we got some snacks.
Then we went back to get Copper.
We were in luck; they were
home. Copper was small, but
he was cute. His mother's
fur was pretty. His sister was very
sick; she had a disease he could
I was really excited when we
got Copper. I held him and
took him out to the truck.
He was really squirmy, He
He climed out and on to the seat
and sat down. Then copper
started whinning. Soon
we got to our grandmother's
and took Copper out of the truck because
he had to go to the
bathroom out doors. As soon as
we got home, Copper started chasing
the cats.

Figure 7–7

Final draft of Andrea's dog piece.

10-30, &-

My New Dog   finah
My dog likes to bite; he
likes to bark and growl.
When you get too close to him,
he bites hard.
. He likes to chase the
cats, but the cats don't like
it. He bites them, too. He likes
to play with his toys, like
the toy bone. He runs for the
door when we come home.
. He is a quarter Irish
Setter and a quarter Golden
Retriever. He weighs 13 Pounds
and he's six weeks old. He's
not small for a puppy.
His name is Copper, that
is the color of him. My mother
named him. We were thinking
alot for his name, but it wasn't
easy. Then the other day my
mom thought of a name for
him — COPPER!

In the final copy of the piece about her new dog (Figure 7–7), written in the beginning of sixth grade, Andrea writes like an outsider, recording the facts. In the one about the day she got her dog (Figure 7–8), written at the end of the sixth grade, she is in the piece. She is excited; she is holding a squirmy puppy. Here, Andrea showed growth as a writer; she made a major revision over time.

The other major type of revision I tried to teach Andrea was to look for places where more specific vocabulary or phrasing could be used. My purpose was for her to use the most appropriate or sophisticated language that she was capable of writing. My leading questions for all new pieces were: Who is your audience for this piece? What is your purpose for writing this? These questions frequently lead to additions and language substitutions. I also asked questions such as: Are there any other ways that you can say this? Are there some other words for———that you could use here? In a group conference, questions like these led to suggestions from other students, as well as responses from Andrea. She usually recorded their suggestions and chose accordingly.

Figure 7–8

A later piece by Andrea about the day she got her dog.

The Day I Got Copper   May 26, 198_

We went to Bristol to get my dog Copper. When we first went there, nobody was home. So we went to a near-by store, and we got some snacks. Then we went back to get Copper. We were in luck; they were home.

Copper was small, but he was cute. His mother's fur was pretty. His sister was very sick; she had a disease. I was really excited when we got Copper.

I held him and took him out to the truck. He was really squirmy. He climbed out and on to the seat and sat down. Then Copper started whinning. Soon we got to our grandmother's and took Copper out of the truck because he had to go to the bathroom. Outdoors. As soon as we got home, Copper started chasing the cats.

Process conferences and interviews

Along with keeping copies of all of Andrea's writing, observing her writing behaviors, asking her about her writing processes, and reflecting on my observations and her talk in my log, I conducted interviews with Andrea at regular intervals as part of my case study research. I wanted to gain a sense of what she saw happening with her writing. The effect of formally interviewing Andrea, as well as informally asking process questions about her pieces, was that Andrea became more conscious of what she was doing and why. As Mary Ellen Giacobbe (1983) has said, "Children grow because they become aware of what they are doing, and then forge on to tackle new issues in their composing."

Throughout Andrea's fifth-grade year, I asked her who the audience was for each piece. Initially, she copied the topics and audiences that her friends had chosen, or she said that the piece was for herself or her mother. Later, she began to write for friends or to share with classmates. By the end of the year, she was writing for or to businesses, authors, other relatives, teachers, and friends and classmates. During quarterly conferences that year, Andrea always stated that spelling was the easiest part of the process for her. Each quarter she designated the hardest part of writing as follows:

1. "Getting ideas down and straight."
2. "Getting all the information and including everything."
3. "Organizing my ideas."
4. "Revising."

When I first asked Andrea what one has to do in order to be a good writer, she said that one has to "know letter forms and make sentences." (I could tell that our sentence-combining exercises of the year before had had an effect.) About midyear she included "thinking of topics and getting ideas down" in her response. In the spring, she said that a good writer "thinks, makes notes, drafts, revises, writes final copies, proofreads, and illustrates."

At regular conferences, I repeatedly asked Andrea what she liked about her piece. She most often replied that she liked the topic, but she sometimes would select out a part that she had worked on particularly hard. At quarterly conferences, I always asked what piece or pieces Andrea liked best. It was difficult for her to choose because she liked most of her pieces, with a few exceptions. Since she invested so much, each piece held a special significance for her. For the entire first year she was unable to say why. She simply shrugged and said, "I just do." During the second year of the writing project and our study, she could attach reasons, stating answers like "I like this letter because I got an answer to it," and "I like this poem best because it says just what I want it to say."

During interviews, I always asked: "How do you feel about your writing?" "Are you a writer?" To the first question she gave the following series of answers as time went by:

"I feel good about what I write."

"I enjoy it."

"I am getting better."

"Good!"

"I wrote forty-two pieces this year."

And to the second question she always answered yes, but her understanding of what it meant to be a writer grew from one who knows how to form cursive letters to one who understands the writing process, from its general application to her specific use of it.

Some outcomes

By law, students in special education are to be reevaluated every three years. In order to update the testing done with Andrea in the third grade, the school psychologist did a psychoeducational evaluation of Andrea in the spring of her sixth-grade year. He found a marked improvement in all cognitive areas, most notably in memory and abstract reasoning. The reasons for this growth are many and complex. I believe that one major factor has been writing, specifically using the process/conference approaches. It allowed Andrea, the learner, to take charge of her learning, to think, to choose, and to evaluate. I know Andrea has grown as a language user, as a writer, and as a student. And that is encouraging indeed.

References

Giacobbe, Mary Ellen. 1981. "Who Says That Children Can't Write the First Week of School?" In *Donald Graves in Australia,* edited by R. D. Walshe. Rozelle, Australia: Primary English Teaching Association. Distributed in the USA by Heinemann Educational Books, Portsmouth NH.

———. 1983. Comment made during the Boothbay Writing Project training sessions, Boothbay Harbor, Maine.

Graves, Donald H. 1983. *Writing: Teachers and Children at Work.* Portsmouth, NH: Heinemann.

Moffett, James. 1981. "Integrity in the Teaching of Writing." In *Coming on Center.* Portsmouth, NH: Boynton/Cook.

8. Remembering Bernice

Patricia Tefft Cousin

As I reflect on my years as a teacher and remember particular students, Bernice always comes to mind. I visualize Bernice: her long, black, curly hair in braids, her light brown skin, her cautious smile. I hear her mischievous laugh, and I see her at different ages—at seven, at ten, and at twelve. Bernice followed me through my teaching career. As busing plans were shifted and changed, my teaching assignment and Bernice's assigned school always coincided. I first met Bernice as a second grader in my self-contained special education class. Bernice's first-grade year had been disastrous. Cerebral palsy caused a minor tremor that affected Bernice's large and small motor proficiency. Difficulties with language also contributed to the problems she had with learning. Interestingly, the psychologists never felt that they were able to get a valid IQ score on Bernice. It was as if Bernice recognized that such an instrument could never measure what she was.

Bernice at seven

It was an early September day, and Bernice and I sat together at a table in the classroom. I was just beginning to implement a writing-process program, and I had asked Bernice to draw a picture and write a story about her picture. After she finished, I looked at her product. As a novice in the area of analyzing early writing, her drawing and writing looked like scribbles to me. Deciphering her written name was impossible. As we talked about her story, Bernice's interests seemed more typical of a three or four year old. This is where we began—Bernice was learning how to communicate through written language and I was learning how to best support her learning. Bernice and I spent the year together drawing pictures, writing stories, and reading books. By the end of the school year, Bernice had made significant progress. She enjoyed literacy-related experiences and began to make some attempts at composing stories on her own. She wrote her name and would often make lists of the names of family members. As Bernice became more involved in literacy, her behavior problems decreased.

I was also a learner that year. As I worked with Bernice, she provided many demonstrations for me—demonstrations of how reading and writing become important to students and how they come to understand that written language makes sense. I observed how Bernice had to learn how to make connections between her personal experiences and how print could be used to tell about these experiences. Using that understanding as a basis, she could then understand how print was used to tell of the experiences of others. I also learned how students develop their understandings of both the functions and forms of written language.

Bernice at nine

After spending a year on sabbatical leave, I began the next year at a new school and heard about an unruly and difficult fourth grader who I was to work with that year. I was surprised to find out that the other teachers were talking about Bernice! And she was certainly surprised to find that I was her teacher again! As I began working with her I noticed from her work folder that she had spent the previous year using a linguistic reading program. I wondered if Bernice had had difficulties with this program, as it was based on a very different view of the language process than I had emphasized with her.

As we began working together again, I asked Bernice to write a story and illustrate it. She drew pictures of two people and then told me that she could not write. I reminded her that she composed stories for me at the other school. After much deliberation, she wrote "cat," "cat," "rat," "fat," paused a moment, and then added "rat," "cat," "rat." She then drew some cats and rats at the bottom of her picture and said that she was finished. (Her "story" is shown in Figure 8–1.) When I asked Bernice to read her story, she read the words written on the page and handed me the story with a big grin on her face.

Bernice produced what she thought I wanted and based that decision on her most recent instructional experience. She produced what she thought the context demanded, along with satisfying her own idea of making sense. She knew that her initial picture did not match the words that she had written, so she added the drawings of the cats and rats after rereading her writing. She appeared satisfied with that strategy and her text in general. She matched picture with text and wrote according to the model of the linguistic program. Bernice made a sophisticated observation of what was expected in the instructional setting and complied accordingly. I had not expected that Bernice would be so attuned to the focus of the language program. This demonstration was a significant one for me. Although I had read research discussing how students assume the language model of the teacher (Harste and Burke 1978), I was not prepared for such a powerful affirmation of it. I easily assumed that Bernice and students with similar problems did not particularly attend to what was happen-

Figure 8–1

Bernice's "story."

ing in the classroom, yet here was strong evidence that Bernice had learned
exactly what had been taught.

After a month of daily writing, Bernice began to write and illustrate simple
stories. She sometimes used syntax similar to that in the linguistic program.
However, she began to convey information of concern to her, and similar to her
work of two years before, her stories and writing focused on herself and her
family. In these situations, she focused on communicating ideas rather than
writing only words that she knew how to spell or words that she could copy
from a reader. Unfortunately, Bernice transferred to another school in mid-
October. In cleaning out her desk, I found many short stories with illustrations
all similar in content and style. (One of these illustrations is shown in Figure
8–2.) As I perused her stories, I realized that Bernice wrote independently now.
I often wondered about Bernice's progress, unable to know that I'd have the
opportunity to find out.

Figure 8–2

One of Bernice's illustrations. "This is Bernice."

Bernice at eleven

The following school year, I transferred to a middle school in the midcity area. One late winter morning, one of the fifth-grade teachers knocked at my resource door. As I opened the door, there stood the teacher with Bernice. And so we began again.

I worked with Bernice during the rest of her fifth-grade year and during her sixth-grade year. By this time, Bernice had developed an interest in reading predictable books and fairy tales and writing stories. The texts that Bernice now produced communicated her ideas in both a more complex and conventional manner. While her main topics still involved family and friends, she no longer used the syntax of the preprimer. As I observed Bernice writing, she appeared to know what she wanted to say and then did so. I compared this with her previous behavior of drawing a picture and then writing a story to match the picture. Bernice no longer needed this strategy to organize her thoughts. She seemed to be rehearsing her ideas mentally rather than with an illustration. While she still illustrated her work, she did so after she had written her text.

Bernice's texts also seemed to be more reflective of her "voice." Now eleven years old, she often wrote of altercations with her mother, a typical concern with middle schoolers. She also used writing to deal with immediate tasks. The sample in Figure 8–3 shows how she used writing to tell another student, a boy, that she was not interested in "going with him."

Figure 8–3

Bernice's note to a boy classmate. "I don't want you to be my boyfriend cause I have another boyfriend."

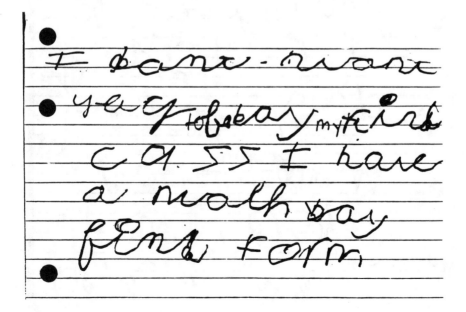

Bernice's writing also now showed the influence of what she had been reading. During the spring of the sixth-grade year, Bernice wrote a story after reading a set of texts about a character called "monster." Bernice's rough draft and final draft are shown in Figures 8–4 and 8–5.

While Bernice's writing looked very dissimilar to that of her age peers, it communicated her message as well as indicated that she was also learning the appropriate use of the conventions of writing. By the end of her sixth year,

Figure 8–4

First draft of Bernice's "monster" text.

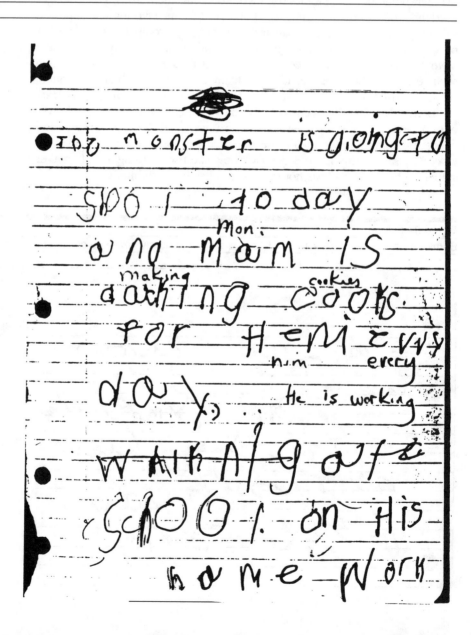

Bernice had found reading to be a recreational activity. She was beginning to develop the basic literacy skills needed to function in our society and understood that she could use language to accomplish needed tasks.

I learned many things about teaching and about learning from Bernice. During her six years of school, Bernice transferred seven times. She had been exposed to diverse and inconsistent views of reading and writing. Her learning

---

Figure 8–5

Final draft of Bernice's "monster" text. "The Monster is going to school today. His Mommy is making cookies for him every day. He is working on his homework. By Bernice."

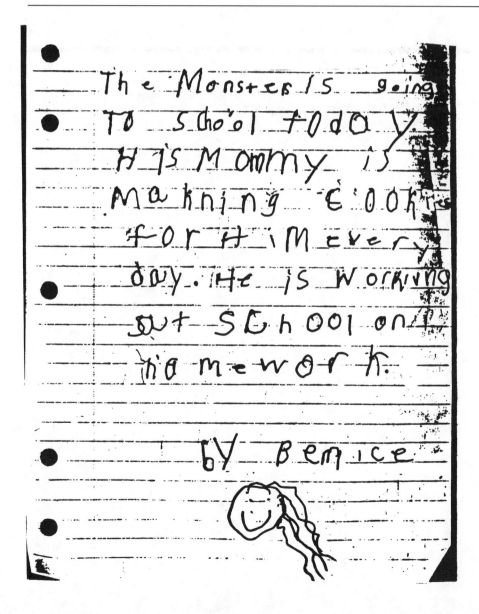

and language difficulties often created additional constraints as she struggled to become literate. Yet Bernice, in her own way, accomplished the goal we have for all learners—to become a reader and a writer and to use those tools to learn about her world. In addition, Bernice, like all authors, found pleasure in the process of composing and in sharing her published work with her peers and other teachers.

My work with Bernice strongly confirmed my belief that most children desire to become literate and will accomplish this in spite of vast difficulties and challenges. A friend of mine remarked that my work with Bernice became a catalyst for me to learn more about language and language difficulties. We can often think that the students are the only learners in a class. As I reflect on my years with Bernice, I believe that I probably benefited the most from our interactions.

References

Harste, Jerome, and Carolyn Burke. 1978. "Towards a Socio-Psycholinguistic Model of Reading Comprehension." *Viewpoints* 54:9–34.

Smith, Frank. 1988. "What the Brain Does Well." Address given at California State University, San Bernardino, CA.

9. Nazar

M. Joan Throne

"It's mine!"

"No, it's not! It's mine!"

Their yelling began to sound serious. I looked up from the papers on my desk, angered at the interruption. "Bo, Mark, come here right now and tell me what is going on."

Mark, inches shorter and pounds lighter, reached me first. The large Nerf ball squashed between his chest and his thin arms, he stood his ground. "I won the game. I'm leader, so the ball is mine!"

Exasperated, I stood up, my patience at an end. "Give that ball to me! This is the last time I'm going to let you play Silent Speed Ball in the room on a rainy day. Who do you think I am, anyway. King Solomon?"

Finally reaching my desk, Bo, undaunted by my outburst, turned toward Mark. His arms outstretched, he issued his final warning, "You just better give that ball to me."

As Mark considered his options, his grip on the ball slackened. I saw my opportunity and grabbed the ball away from him. Having reached my decision, I proclaimed my verdict: "I am going to cut this thing in half and you can each have a half." At that I heard someone begin to laugh. I looked around the room for the culprit and saw that Nazar, my Pakistani student, was nearly doubled over with laughter.

"Nazar, do you know that story?" Since I knew his politeness would prevent him from laughing simply because I'd blown my cool, I concluded that he was reacting to my biblical reference. It surprised me that he could relate what had happened with Bo and Mark to the Old Testament story about King Solomon's solution to the argument two women were having over a baby. He nodded his head vigorously and continued laughing. Almost immediately I joined him, seeing some humor in the situation myself, and the entire class breathed a sigh of relief.

Nazar seldom spoke to me in English. I knew he understood much of what he heard, but understanding the subtleties behind that exchange with Bo and Mark meant he understood far more than I imagined. I found it hard to believe that this was the same student who walked into the room so hesitantly five months earlier.

We were into our second week of school when Nazar entered our sixth-grade class near the middle of the day. Except for Bo, he was taller than the other boys, had dark hair and eyes, and was a little on the heavy side. I helped him locate a desk that suited his larger frame and introduced him to Stephen, Mark, and Jason, who were getting ready for lunch. "Ask Nazar to go to lunch with you," I suggested.

Jason tried. "Come with us. It's time for lunch." Nazar shook his head.

"He won't come with us," Mark reported, as the three of them headed out the door.

Thinking that he didn't understand, I pretended to be eating and pointed to the doorway. He continued to shake his head. "Nazar, it's time for lunch. Come with me," I coaxed. Nazar remained firmly planted in his seat.

About a week later he wrote in his dialogue journal, "I do not feel hungry when the hole class dines." He continued to eat alone in the room for about three weeks. Then, one day Bo announced, "Nazar's eating lunch with us today!" Sure enough, Nazar courageously left the security of our classroom and ventured into that place of noise and confusion, the cafeteria. I saw him there, his head buried in his lunchbox, glancing up now and then like a frightened chipmunk ready to scamper away at the first sign of trouble. That picture contrasts sharply with my picture of him nearer the end of the year playing paper football across the cafeteria table with his friends, Todd, Bo, and Jason.

For the second year in a row, my sixth-grade, self-contained class included seven ESL students from seven different countries. I felt I needed to know more about how students learn a second language and decided to keep a journal that would focus on my beginning ESL student, Nazar, and his growth as a writer.

There was a time when I didn't enjoy teaching language arts. In fact, I preferred teaching math. I couldn't see how students could transfer the isolated skills they were learning to real reading and real writing. I didn't see how reading most of the stories in the basals could convince students that reading was fun, and I suspected that all those red marks I was putting on their stories taught them next to nothing about writing. I was confused about how to teach reading and writing.

Reading Nancie Atwell's book *In the Middle* (1987) convinced me to do what I should have done years ago. I put the basals, language texts, and workbooks in storage and encouraged my students to select and to write about books they wanted to read. I encouraged them to write on topics they chose and began helping them learn the mechanics of writing within the context of the pieces they wrote. They began meeting with each other for help during writing workshop, and, at the end of the workshop, they began sharing their stories with the entire class or in small groups. Today my students share in the responsibility for their own learning and their classmates' learning not only in language arts but in all subject areas. Observing and listening to my students have taught me far more about teaching than any course I've taken.

I knew that through observing Nazar I could learn much about how to help my beginning ESL students learn to write in a second language. County regulations mandated that an ESL specialist work with him, so he left the room to work with a special teacher almost every day. In the beginning, he saw the specialist for two hours a day. Then in December, because of the progress he was making and because of my constant inquiries, that was cut to one hour. Though scheduling problems prevented his ESL teacher from coming to the room to work with him, we often talked about his progress in learning English. We were both working to help him with vocabulary development, spelling, and writing, but I knew that if he became an active participant in my classroom, his classmates would become invaluable as teachers of his second language.

One of the first things Nazar needed to do if he was to become an active participant in the classroom was to become acquainted with his classmates and with me and to learn he could trust us. Once trust had been established, I thought Nazar would be much more willing to take the risks that would involve making mistakes but are so important to growth in learning a language.

Dialogue journals

I decided to use a dialogue journal as a way for the two of us to become acquainted and as a way to convince him that he could trust me (Staton, Peyton, and Gutstein 1986). In previous years, I found dialogue journals invaluable. No matter where the students were academically, they could write to me in their journals. They were free to write about whatever interested them knowing that I wouldn't correct their mistakes.

Thanks to his helpful uncle who knew some English, Nazar almost immediately understood what I meant by a dialogue journal. Within two days of being in our class, I learned two important things about Nazar through his journal. On September 21, he wrote, "Yes I Do like my School very much and I will like to play kickball."

Late in September I tried to encourage him to take risks. We were discussing, in his journal, reasons for eating and for not eating in the cafeteria. He had told me that he didn't want to eat there because he didn't feel hungry at that time. In my response, I said that the cafeteria was a good place to talk with the other students. He wrote, "OK Madam I will try to Mix with other students but the problem with me is the language." On September 26, I wrote that if I moved to Pakistan I would need lots of help to learn the language. I told him that the students wanted to help him, and that I was happy that he would try to mix with them. Then I added, "Do not be afraid to make mistakes!"

On October 14, I explained in a journal entry that he did not need to worry about spelling, and he wrote about the problem he saw in that proposal. "Madam, alright I will write the words as they would sound to me But still I fear I might not become habitual of writing wrong spelling because there are many words which do'not as they sound."

I learned so much about Nazar through the journal. When he wrote and told me that he'd received a new bicycle on October 25, I asked him if he would be riding it to school, and his answer told me that he couldn't because he and his brother were responsible for taking their two sisters to school. Through his journal, I learned in October that Nazar wanted to understand the meaning of trick or treating, that he was having a problem with another student, and that it pleased him to know his house was close to mine. He also graciously invited me to his house for tea. By the end of March, we were having the kind of conversations friends often have:

"Dear Nazar, What is the best part of your day? I think eating is the best part of my day. I am trying to lose weight, and all I think about is food! food! food! Mrs. T."

"Dear Mrs. T. My best part is match. I like math. your weight is not very much. I don't lik very much food because if I eat very much my weight is very havy. I want I lose my weight."

We continued our conversation about food and weight with Nazar, always the gentleman, writing:

"I try to lose my some weight. Now I am very havy . . . You don't want lose your weight because you looks better. Now I understand math before I don't know then Adam help me in math."

Becoming acquainted with peers

By March, Nazar was giving help to and receiving help from his friends. Earlier in the year I had been concerned because he didn't seem to have any friends. He seldom spoke in English to me or to his classmates. For a trusting relationship to develop with his classmates, I felt that Nazar needed to become more confident in using spoken English. I had to do more than just tell him to "talk." Nazar needed to be in a situation where talking was for a purpose (Johnson 1988).

In November, I realized our hands-on approach in science might create the opportunity to use English. In the November unit, "Bulbs and Batteries," students worked together to investigate lighting the bulbs using wires and batteries, then they drew pictures to show what they tried. I paired Nazar with Todd, one of my more talkative students, then watched and listened as they struggled to solve the problem of how to light the bulb, often communicating through touching and motioning. "This is the way it works," Todd insisted. "This!" Nazar said. As I watched, I soon realized that Nazar understood what he was doing and was able to help Todd, but he said very little.

At the end of one of the sessions, Nazar and Todd joined the rest of the students, all crowding around one desk, taping their batteries together, determined to discover how many batteries it would take to blow out a bulb. Nazar had been successful in making new friends and in learning more about the workings of bulbs and batteries, but it did not seem that I had been very successful in my plan to encourage him to talk.

In looking back over my journal, however, I noticed that it was just four days after working with Todd in science that Nazar began volunteering answers in math. I noticed, too, that it was about that time that Todd's head was often bent with Nazar's as they read his dialogue journal. Nazar was obviously receiving some help from Todd in understanding my entries.

The writing workshop

Hansen (1987) said that it is the response among children that "keeps their writing and reading going" (42). Though I was his audience in reading his journal entries, I was not one of Nazar's peers. I felt it was important for him to write and to share his writing with his peers. Since he knew very little English in September, I encouraged him to write his stories in his native language, Urdu. At the end of September, Nazar wrote and, to my surprise, shared a story in Urdu. The students were fascinated. They wanted to see how his writing looked and asked to hear the story again. Nazar learned that day that he had brought something of value to us, the ability to read, write, and speak in another language.

Late in October, he wrote one of his first stories in English. He titled it "The Cow." It had a simple structure, probably a pattern he had learned in his ESL class, but it was a beginning. "The cow useful and fathful animal It has two ear It has two eyes It has two harns It has four legs It has long tail It has one mouth It colour is defrint clour black and white It eats grass."

Then on November 22, soon after working with Todd in science, Nazar told me that he was writing a story about his friend Todd. He wrote, "My friend name is Todd. He is a good boy. Todd is in six grade He is my class fellow. we are play together. He is help for me reading He help for me math. He help for me everytime. Me like Todd." Nazar shared his story with Todd, who had helped him with it and who was very pleased to be the focus of his friend's story.

Early in December, after I had received permission for Nazar to remain in the room for an hour more every day, he began writing on a variety of topics. He wrote stories about fun times with his friend, a dog he left in Pakistan, and his father's trip to New York. On December 12, he wrote a story about schools in Pakistan that explained, at least in part, his hesitancy about speaking in English. He wrote, "In Pakistan school is very different because pakistan school no sports. Math is not eazy. No library. No Music, and no cumputers. No in class movie. only book read and rite. In Pakistan Schools teachers hit children Because somebdy no write home work or work in mastake. In Pakistan only woman teachers."

Nazar's classmates were interested in learning more about life in Pakistan. Their interest inspired him to write a piece for our class magazine's special edition *Traditions*. The edited version follows. "On August 14, all Pakistanis have a holiday. All the schools and offices are closed. On that day, in 1947, Pakistan became a new nation. To celebrate that special day, all the houses in Pakistan display the Pakistani flag. In the evening, all the houses display different colored lights, green, red, blue, yellow, and other colors. During that day, people go visiting. Some children go to an uncle's house. Children play different games. This is a very happy day!"

Calkins (1986) said, "The content of the writing workshop is the content of real life, for the workshop begins with what each student thinks, feels, and experiences, and with the human urge to articulate and understand experience" (8). This was never more apparent to me than on January 13. After lunch Nazar asked me if it was time for writing. I said, "Yes," but I was a little confused. He would always write in workshop, but had never been quite so eager for it to begin. Then I remembered how excited he'd been in the morning talking with Bo and Mark. He had been using his new language more in conversation with his friends, but this morning he had been especially talkative. Knowing sixth graders rather well, I asked, "Were you in a fight?" He smiled and said, "Not me, I watch."

Nazar wrote his longest story so far that day, and it didn't seem to take much time for him to write it. It contrasted sharply with the "cow" story he had written in October. He wrote, "Yester I go after school home. and my friend David say, you come watch me Some boy, fight me and my other friend . . . David and Kevin go fight boy. David say I fight you in play no real fight. They say ok we fight in play . . . boy one punch face of Nabeel . . . after Kevin say . . . you fight real, I don't fight you." When he finished writing, he invited Adam to a conference corner to hear his story.

On February 9, he read a story he had written in English for the first time in a large-group share: "I have three friend. My friend names is Stephen, Todd, David. My friend help me in the study. Todd help me in math and Stephen help me in saince and David help me in Inglish. Todd and Stephen in my class. Todd and Stephen sit with me. David is not in my class. Todd Stephen and David is my very good friend."

The students were eager to respond to Nazar's sharing. Mark said, "I like how you wrote and how you explained that David wasn't in our class and how each person helped." Angela asked, "Did you write your story in English?" Adam complained, "I'm your friend too!" Stephen said, "I like the way you wrote about your friends and how you explained why each was your friend." The students obviously wanted to encourage Nazar. That they were successful could be seen in his smiles and his sparkling dark eyes.

On February 14, I asked Nazar to tell me what helped him learn English. He wrote, "This things help me learn in English. Spalling help me in learn English. Sentenses help me learn in English. Somebody taking [talking] with me and Diologue jurnal help me learn in English. I read books This help me. Some body taking and I lesson This help me in learn English." More and more often I noticed Nazar looking up from his writing to ask Bo, Todd, or one of his other friends for help when he was stuck on a word or had a question about his writing.

Then he shared again on February 23. He'd had some trouble thinking of a topic for writing. When I conferenced with him, I suggested he write in Urdu. I thought maybe that would help the ideas begin to flow. My suggestion seemed to help. He had probably heard the story he wrote, about a lion and a rat, in his native country. The lion did a good deed for the rat, and the rat returned the favor. He shared his story with the entire group, first in Urdu, then in English. It was interesting to all of us to hear the same story in both languages.

During the next several weeks he spent some time translating into English stories he had written earlier in the year in Urdu. He also wrote stories about his family, an accident he had witnessed, what he did after school, and a new house he was moving into in April. He wrote a story that was probably a retelling of a story he had heard in Pakistan about a father and his five sons. The five sons were fighting and the father taught them a lesson using five sticks. He told each son to give him a stick. He put the sticks together, then told his sons to break them. They couldn't. Next he gave each son one stick and told them to break their sticks. They all broke their sticks. The father said that when they are together, nobody can break them. When they are not together, everybody can break them. After that the sons stopped fighting.

A special day in the writing workshop

Since our school was one of the first in the area to implement a whole-language process approach in reading and writing, we had many visitors. The students became used to having strangers in the room asking them questions, especially about their writing. In fact, they became far more used to it than I did. On March 14 the assistant principal called me at home to ask, "Would you mind having your class videotaped for public broadcasting tomorrow? They are interested in how kids share and respond to each other." Though I found the idea frightening, I said yes. I knew by now that nothing worked so well as audience to inspire writing.

The next morning I announced to my class, "We are having special visitors today. A TV crew will be here this afternoon to do some taping for public broadcasting." The excitement began to build, and I stopped talking. When the noise died down, I continued, "They are interested in how we share and respond to each other. We will have both large- and small-group share today. You will need to share something you've written or something you've read. We'll have workshop this morning so you'll have time to make your selection."

Some of my students began looking through writing folders to select something to share, while others began writing and reading. Nazar told me he wanted to share his story about the father and his five sons. Near the end of the workshop, just before lunch, I asked for volunteers to share with the large group when we began our afternoon's adventure. Stephen, Laura, Tammy, and Thanh hesitantly volunteered. As we were leaving for lunch, we saw the TV crew with their lights, cameras, microphones, and cables walking toward our room. The kids lost their appetites, but I insisted that they have lunch.

Finally, lunch and break were over, the lights were in place, and the cameras were ready. I began, "We are going to have large-group share today. Remember when you respond, be kind." I paused, then continued, "Who will volunteer to read his or her paper?" About half the hands in the room went up. I tried to remember my volunteers and called on Stephen. He walked to the writer's stool, sat down, and tried to ignore the boom mike dangling over his head as he read his paper. When he finished, the kids responded, kindly yet helpfully, just as though we'd practiced.

After the students had finished sharing with the large group, the small groups met for their sharing time. We don't usually have both on the same day, but today was an exception. By the time it was Nazar's turn to read his story to his group, we were wiping the sweat off our faces. The heat from the lights, plus a warm, near-spring day, made the room uncomfortable. But the kids didn't complain. Nazar shared his story, about the father and his sons, first in his native language, then in English. I didn't hear the immediate response to his sharing because of a problem on the other side of the room. I got back to Nazar's group in time to hear the interviewer ask, "What makes this class different?" Bo, never at a loss for words, said, "We help each other."

Finally, the crew wound up cables, packed their equipment, thanked me for permitting them to videotape us, and left. "Upper-level students are dismissed," was announced over the intercom, and I walked to the doorway to say good-bye to a rather animated group of students. Nazar met his friend David just outside our room, and I could hear them talking excitedly together as they walked down the hallway.

Mentally and physically exhausted, I walked back into the soothing quiet of my room. As I relaxed on the chair behind my desk thinking over the activities of the day, my thoughts went back to that day when Nazar first walked into our room, a tall, dark-haired boy, a little on the heavy side. Somehow it had happened. He had become an active participant in this wonderful community of learners I call my class.

References

Atwell, Nancie. 1987. *In the Middle: Reading, Writing, and Learning with Adolescents*. Portsmouth, NH: Boynton/Cook.

Calkins, Lucy McCormick. 1986. *The Art of Teaching Writing*. Portsmouth, NH: Heinemann.

Hansen, Jane. 1987. *When Writers Read*. Portsmouth, NH: Heinemann.

Johnson, Donna. 1988. "ESL Children as Teachers: A Social View of Second Language Use." *Language Arts* 65:154–163.

Staton, Jana, Joy Kreeft Peyton, and Shelley Gutstein, eds. 1986. "Dialogue Journals in ESL Settings." *Dialogue* 3 (2):1–12. Washington DC: Center for Applied Linguistics.

10. The Student with Learning Disabilities in a Writing-Process Classroom

William L. Wansart

Jessica is a student with learning disabilities. In April, she signed up to share the last book she would publish during her fourth-grade year. Sitting at her desk that morning, she told a classmate, Mike, that she did not want to share the book because she felt she could not read very well. Mike looked at her with surprise and said, "Jessica, you don't have to read, *you* can *write!*" (emphasis his). He grabbed the book from her saying, "I'll read it for you," but she took it back, laughing, and later read it to the class herself.

This was Jessica's most successful whole-class sharing experience all year. After she read, there were immediate questions about her ideas and many comments about how much she knew about animals, about the humor in the story, and about the parts the class liked best. One student, responding to the various details about animals in the story, inquired, "I got to ask. Why do you like facts, so many facts?" Before Jessica could answer, another student yelled out, "Because she knows so much about them."

As Jessica returned to her desk, the teacher initiated a transition to reading time, asking one of the students to hand out reading folders. However, as her reading folder was placed on her desk, Jessica whispered to herself, "I want to write some more!"

Jessica was not always as confident or as interested in writing as this story indicates. For the first four months of the school year, she had rarely spoken and had only written when it was required. Jessica attended the resource room two hours per day for remediation in reading, math, and writing. Although she remained in her regular classroom during the daily writing time, she did not meet in small groups like the others and, other than listening, did not participate in class discussions of students' writing. Jessica needed a great deal of assistance in the resource room just to write a few sentences in the reading journal that was required in her regular class. She would stare at the floor, saying little, while the resource room teacher aide prodded her into writing one or two sentences. Jessica wrote in oversized manuscript letters, usually ignoring all writing conventions and spelling almost completely phonetically.

How could Jessica have changed so much by the end of the school year? Her immersion in a classroom society that valued the process of writing and collaborative problem solving was essential to her progress. Jessica's regular classroom was unusual in that the teacher used writing process (Graves 1983) and reading process (Hansen 1987) as the primary instructional approaches. Writing process establishes a set of conditions under which students and teachers work, focusing on both the meaning of the writing and the abilities of the writer. Students learn to first clarify their ideas so that they can communicate what they know to their teacher and to the other students. Then, within the context of meaningful ideas, the conventions of writing can be applied. Such a focus changes the way students and teachers interact with one another and fosters independent learning.

As the popularity of process-oriented writing has increased, both regular and special education teachers have voiced concerns over whether this type of instruction can meet the needs of students with reading and writing disabilities. To address this question, a year-long participant observation was conducted in a New Hampshire elementary school. This predominantly middle-class school, which serves 375 students in grades one through six, had been using the writing-process approach in all its classrooms for the previous four years.

The observational technique employed in this study has been described by Graves (1984) and is analogous with the methodology of the preliminary field-work phase in the ethnography of communication research tradition described by Jacob (1987). It involved weekly observation of the verbalizations and behaviors of the students and teacher in a single fourth-grade classroom as they interacted during reading and writing instruction. Students were informally interviewed to provide explanations for various behaviors and activities. Jessica was chosen as a case study and was observed carefully in the classroom and the resource room. The teacher acted as a research collaborator; she made observations of Jessica during the other four school days and described them to the researcher. All observations, kept in field note form, were analyzed and categorized weekly. Photocopies were kept of as much of the written material Jessica produced during the year as possible. In January, Jessica's time in the resource room was reduced to thirty minutes a day, for math remediation only, so that she could participate fully with her peers in the regular classroom. She no longer received resource room assistance with her writing difficulties.

The purpose of this study was to develop a description of what Jessica learned about writing and reading, as well as a description of the classroom context within which this learning occurred. The context included the social and instructional interactions between the teacher and the students, as well as among the students themselves, with an emphasis on the interactions between normally achieving students and those with learning disabilities.

Critical elements of the writing-process approach

An analysis of the observational data revealed four categories of classroom experience that appeared to be critical elements in Jessica's growth as a writer:

(a) a sense of a community of learners, (b) control of one's writing, (c) collaborative and independent problem solving, and (d) opportunities for generalization and transfer of learning. These categories encompass many of the features identified by Graves (1985) and Bos (1988) as important considerations for teaching writing to students with learning disabilities. Together they created a powerful environment in Jessica's classroom, an environment in which Jessica learned to trust her own knowledge and to become a better writer.

A sense of community.   Perhaps the most important feature of a writing-process classroom is the sense of community. It is from this community of writers, sharing the struggle of learning to communicate through the written word, that the skills of writing develop. The community emerges from the studio setting (Graves 1983), which includes (a) daily sustained writing time, (b) individual writing conferences between students, and (c) sharing of both work-in-progress and published pieces with the whole class. According to Graves (1983) and Calkins (1986) it is important for students to expect to have at least 45 minutes a day, four days a week to work on their writing. Published pieces are those that have been corrected for content and conventions with the help of the teacher and then copied over, without error, and bound in book form with illustrations.

The community milieu supports the idea that writing is hard work for everyone. This sense of community allows students with writing disabilities to become integrated into the classroom learning process and to feel a connection with other students, rather than feeling isolated and incapable.

In Jessica's classroom, students could frequently overhear one another discussing their writing with the teacher or with another student. During one observation, Jessica looked up from her writing as Brandy asked the teacher for help. After discussing the problem a moment, the teacher suggested that Brandy confer with another student, Jody. The teacher told Jody that Brandy was "stuck," and the two students moved to a corner of the room, where Brandy began by telling Jody, "I need your help!"

On another occasion, the teacher sat at a large table between Jessica and Sean, a boy with no apparent writing problems. After discussing the capitalization of proper nouns with Jessica and directing her to make the appropriate corrections on her page, the teacher turned to Sean and began to discuss with him his impressions of his writing progress. Jessica occasionally glanced at them as Sean explained his editing changes. The teacher then mentioned that he had met his goal of consistently using quotation marks.

This type of background dialogue is vital for the student with written language disabilities because it reinforces the idea that writing is a process. At the beginning of the year, Jessica was overly concerned with finishing academic tasks, often producing any product regardless of accuracy or quality as long as the task was completed. As the year progressed, she began to internalize the classroom atmosphere, which valued the process of working and creating writing and deemphasized finished products. Products, in the form of published books, were valued, but no more than the process of creating them. Understanding this important concept eventually enabled Jessica to begin to critically evaluate and improve her own writing.

Control of one's writing.   The empowerment of the writer as a thinking, creative, and autonomous person is an important part of the writing process. Allowing students to choose their own topics and to control the pace of their writing can help accomplish this. In contrast, traditional remedial approaches for students with written language disabilities have emphasized the development of isolated skills through teacher-directed instructional activities. When students write in such a controlled environment, it is usually to achieve an externally determined goal. Often the student experiences little or no connection between this writing and the communication of ideas (Graves 1985).

In a writing-process classroom, students share the responsibility for their progress with the teacher. The students choose the topic, the genre, and whether or not they will continue with a particular piece or begin a new one. The teacher expects that the students will be writing, conferring with the teacher and peers about writing, editing, or publishing a finished piece, but the students retain control of the content and the purpose.

Students with written language disabilities often have little experience setting a purpose for their writing. The following describes Jessica's progress toward taking increasing control of her writing.

Jessica had worked long and hard on a single piece of writing she had begun in September. Months of sustained work had finally produced a 425-word fantasy story about the adventures of a flying horse. Jessica had rarely discussed her work with anyone other than her teacher and had never signed up to share her progress with the class. The teacher let Jessica continue like this, hoping that she would eventually feel the support of the classroom community and would begin to share her work. When she finally published the story in January, she did indeed share it with the class, as required by classroom rules. Among the interesting reactions to her book was the observation by one boy that she had not shown the illustrations while she read. Immediately, two other students shouted together, "She doesn't need to show the pictures, I can see it in my mind." Given the time and control to develop this story at her own pace, Jessica had demonstrated the ability to conjure vivid images with her written words.

Jessica took another two months to write her second story, also on a fantasy topic. However, in contrast to her first writing experience, the class was now interested in her writing. In addition, Jessica was enough a part of the classroom community that the writing of others could influence her. She began a third piece of writing and finished it in four days. It was still about an animal, her pet, but for the first time it was not fantasy. She had made an important change, to a type of writing that the other students referred to as a "real" story: a personal narrative about things occurring in one's own life. She had made this shift to a genre more like that used by the other students on her own accord and in her own time, again demonstrating her increasing control over her own writing.

After publishing the pet story in mid-April, Jessica made another important change. Without a good idea for a new story, she began to write three separate stories, working on all three intermittently. This was common among her normally achieving peers, who would select one story they felt was developing well and finish it for publication. Jessica's three stories were all "real" stories, with one even including herself as a character. In a conference with her teacher in May, Jessica confessed that writing was becoming difficult because she "didn't know how it would end." Jessica's teacher suggested she just write down all the ideas she had, even if they were not in the correct order. Later they could be cut up and pasted together in new ways to put the story together. This was a novel idea for Jessica, and a great strategy to help her in her struggle to communicate using the written word, a struggle that she was increasingly directing herself.

Collaborative and independent problem solving. Both collaborative and independent problem solving are demonstrated in a writing-process classroom. The teacher models the social interactions involved in the process of writing. Discussions with peers are encouraged as a method to solve a variety of problems, such as (a) whether the piece of writing really communicates its intended message, (b) how the piece can be reorganized, and (c) what a good title would be. The collaborative model implies that writing is difficult for everyone at times, even for the teacher who often shares his or her writing, and that everyone needs the help and suggestions of others to succeed. It also implies that solutions to problems exist and that the search for these solutions is at least as important as completing a finished product.

This modeling of the problem-solving process is very important for students with learning disabilities. These students frequently give up after their first failed attempt at academic tasks such as writing because they do not have alternative problem-solving strategies (Hagen, Barclay, and Newman 1982; Paris and Oka 1986). Teacher modeling encourages the use of a variety of strategies, as in the example presented earlier of Jessica watching as Brandy sought help from the teacher, who redirected her to a peer for assistance. This demonstration taught Jessica two things. First, she learned an effective method for solving problems, both her need for help and the particular writing problem. Second, and perhaps more importantly, she learned that the students in the class, and by implication Jessica herself, were capable of solving writing problems. The teacher respected the students' ability to solve problems and valued their ideas.

The conventions required for clear written communication are also modeled in the classroom. From students' writing, the teacher learns what they know about the act of writing itself and about their chosen topics. The teacher can then help the student understand how a new skill, such as spelling, punctuation, or paragraphing, will help them communicate their intent. When the teacher helped Jessica edit for capitalization, she knew that Jessica would understand the need for it now because the capital letters were placed in the context of her own writing.

A broad range of skills and abilities needed for writing are also modeled by the students. In a sense, there are as many teachers as there are individuals in the classroom. When students work with one another, or when they share their writing with the group, a whole range of ideas, styles of writing, and individual problems and solutions are modeled for the class. Through this process, students gain new perspectives on their own writing, discover alternative solutions to mutual problems, and learn new skills and techniques.

The modeling inherent in this collaboration could be seen as Jessica worked on her reading journal one morning. She was having difficulty reading some of the comments the teacher had written about her book, and finally asked another student for help. Brandy and then Kristin came over to Jessica's desk. The ensuing discussion included the following examples of students teaching and modeling writing skills for one another.

Kristin read the teacher's first question out loud. As Jessica wrote the answer, the two helpers read over her shoulder. Brandy suggested an incorrect spelling for a word, and Kristin corrected her. Brandy pointed to the writing and said, "OK, put a period in there." Kristin read the next question, which asked why the ship had exploded. "It was hit by lightning," said Jessica. Then, spontaneously modeling how to expand language, Kristin said, "So say, 'hit by lightening,' say, 'it exploded because it was hit by lightening.' " They all tried to spell "exploded," and Kristin finally found the word in the book Jessica was writing about, which was lying on the desk. Jessica then continued on her own. As Brandy walked away she said, "OK, if you need me you know what to do!"

Opportunities for generalization and transfer. When students write with a purpose, the skills they acquire have meaning. They begin to understand the function of a skill by seeing it used to solve a problem in their own writing, or in the writing of their classmates and teachers (Graves 1984). In such an environment, students are reminded daily of the usefulness of a wide range of strategies and skills, and they begin to generalize them to a broad range of writing problems. The subject of "writing" begins to include all forms of writing, such as reading journals and science project reports. Jessica began to demonstrate generalized use of many of the writing strategies used by her peers in her regular classroom, without deliberate prompting by her teacher. While she had begun the year unable to complete her reading journal without resource room help, she was able, by March, to assume complete responsibility for writing in this journal. In addition, she began to write the answers to science test questions independently, whereas previously, the teacher had had her answer orally. Jessica began to edit her own work and increasingly used correct spelling in initial drafts. In May, she placed a note on her teacher's desk explaining that a pet, who had been the subject of one of her books, had died. Jessica had spontaneously chosen to use writing to communicate this painful message.

Summary

Four categories of experience in a writing-process classroom have been described, which provided a portrait of a writing-process classroom at work. Jessica's experiences suggest that students with learning disabilities can respond very favorably to instruction that focuses on the process of writing and emphasizes what they know rather than focusing on their inadequacies.

Jessica made many important gains during her fourth-grade year. She reached the point where she discovered that she wanted to write, and she had learned many strategies to facilitate that goal. She still had a good deal to learn, such as the correct spelling of many common words, consistent use of capitalization and punctuation, and the concept of paragraphing, but she had reached the point where direct teaching of specific writing skills could be meaningfully connected with her desire to communicate. Jessica had become a writer the day she said, "I want to write."

References

Bos, C. S. 1988. "Process-Oriented Writing: Instructional Implications for Mildly Handicapped Students." *Exceptional Children* 54: 521–527.

Calkins, Lucy M. 1986. *The Art of Teaching Writing*. Portsmouth, NH: Heinemann.

Graves, Donald H. 1983. *Writing: Teachers and Children at Work*. Portsmouth, NH: Heinemann.

———. 1984. *A Researcher Learns to Write*. Portsmouth, NH: Heinemann.

———. 1985. "All Children Can Write." *Learning Disabilities Focus* 1: 36–43.

Hagen, J. W., C. R. Barclay, and R. S. Newman. 1982. "Metacognition, Self-Knowledge, and Learning Disabilities: Some Thoughts on Knowing and Doing." *Topics in Learning and Learning Disabilities* 2: 19–25.

Hansen, Jane. 1987. *When Writers Read*. Portsmouth, NH: Heinemann.

Jacob, E. 1987. "Qualitative Research Traditions: A Review." *Review of Educational Research* 57: 1–50.

Paris, S. G., and E. R. Oka. 1986. "Self-Regulated Learning among Exceptional Children." *Exceptional Children* 53: 103–108.

11. First Things First: Conditions and Connections to Literacy

Susan Stires

It was time for a change a couple of years ago. After eight years as a resource room teacher, I decided to return to general education and teach first grade. However, I discovered I was still functioning as a special education teacher: in my class of twenty children, eight had special needs. Two students were considered to have multiple handicaps; others had emotional or developmental problems; and two had special needs specifically in the area of language development. My challenge was to provide the best learning environment possible for all of my students.

Conditions for language learning in the classroom

In Andrea Butler and Jan Turnbill's book *Towards a Reading-Writing Classroom* (1987), Brian Cambourne presents seven conditions for making meaning through talk successful: immersion, demonstration, expectation, responsibility, approximation, employment, and feedback. He believes that these conditions are relevant to all kinds of language learning and to literacy, and that they are transferable to classroom practice.

My first-grade classroom operated under those seven conditions, for I believe, along with Cambourne, that these conditions are important for all students. Further, I believe they are essential for children with language delays in order for them to be contributing members of the classroom community.

Immersion.   From the time they are born, most children are immersed in meaningful and purposeful language. In my classroom, the students were immersed in meaningful, purposeful language for social and academic reasons. We had a meeting time each morning for sharing orally with each other, and we had reading and writing sharing times as well. Talk surrounded literature, writing, math, science, and social studies. Throughout the day, reading and writing occurred in content studies or was part of reading and writing workshops.

Demonstration.   In learning to talk, children have thousands of demonstrations of using language in functional and meaningful ways. In my classroom, each child had twenty other people providing language and literacy demonstrations to him or her. There were the three formal, whole-group meetings for sharing (oral, reading, and writing) mentioned above. We also shared informally as we collaborated throughout the day. As the teacher, it was my responsibility to provide demonstrations in lessons and conferences. The students often conducted minilessons and engaged in peer conferences. Except for spelling tests, which were mandated, all information was shared.

Expectation.   Parents of young children expect their children to talk. I expected my first graders, including the ones with language difficulties, to write and to read, and they did. My message to children was that reading and writing were pleasurable activities that we could all enjoy. I did not lower my expectations for anyone, but celebrated what each reader/writer could do.

Responsibility.   Children are responsible for their oral language learning— the rate and type of language conventions that they master. My students were similarly responsible for the rate and types of print conventions that they mastered. There were also oral language conventions to master in the classroom, such as how to be a good audience for a writer and a reader, and how to ask questions that will help the writer/reader who is sharing. My role was to give my students choices and to help them take responsibility for their learning.

Approximation.   In most homes, young children's language approximations are not only tolerated but celebrated. When a child begins to pronounce words, parents record their approximations in a baby book; they know that the articulation and language structures will become more conventional with time. In some classrooms, such as mine, reading and writing approximations, like invented spelling, in-head texts (Stires 1988), labeling, and slotting of sentences, are celebrated and used as bases for building literacy. I know what first-grade competence is in general; I learn what it is for each individual.

Employment.   In most cases, children have opportunities for talking and listening during all waking hours. The opportunities to talk, listen, read, and write should be similarly open in the classroom. Numbers necessitated turn-taking in my classroom, but everyone used language continuously in some form.

Feedback.   Parents reflect back to their children the conventional language forms while centering on the meaning that children are making (Heath 1983; Wells 1986). The implication for me as a teacher is that I must do exactly the same thing in my classroom. If I model giving good feedback, my students will give good feedback to each other. I think they did. Since correction was the feedback I received as a learner, and gave for my first ten years as a teacher, I've had to work very hard at responding well.

The two children with language difficulties who entered my class in the fall grew and changed as the year progressed. Their growth was not straightforward or spectacular, but it was constant and real.

Brooke

Brooke was a tall girl with long, straight blonde hair that fell across her face. She wore glasses, but she usually forgot to bring them to school. She was older than many of her classmates because she had spent two years in kindergarten. During her prekindergarten year, she rarely spoke. The school language therapist monitored Brooke's entire class that year, and the following year she monitored Brooke. Although Brooke did not speak in a large group, she did talk to the teacher and to a few of the children during her second year in kindergarten. Both kindergarten teachers described Brooke as making inconsistent progress overall, but her difficulties were seen as developmental.

When Brooke entered first grade, many of her strengths and weaknesses were readily apparent. Her visual skills were good; she loved to draw and had a fine aesthetic sense. She was very organized about the things she kept in her desk, and she often would clean and organize classroom shelves. Socially, she was well liked by her classmates because she loved to play and was willing to follow others' suggestions.

However, Brooke was often confused, not knowing what to do next despite established routines, which were easily learned by children who were more than a year younger than she was. It took a long time for Brooke to distinguish between her reading and writing folders and her math and spelling books. And she required cues from the other children to determine what to do with them, when to get in line for recess and lunch, when to go to meetings at the rug, as well as when to go to art, music, and gym, and even when to go home.

I had Brooke tested by the language therapist in October because she did not speak except to a few other children and a bit to me. She seemed unable to attend to group and individual questions, discussions, and conversation. The testing yielded a picture of a child with limited language abilities. The language therapist recommended that Brooke work with her for forty minutes a week on discriminating sounds and following directions. I agreed because I knew that Brooke's parents were anxious since the extra year to allow for development hadn't solved her language problems, and because I knew that the therapist would provide a context for the activities in the form of games. I also knew that the literate environment of my classroom would nurture Brooke's language development.

At that point, Brooke was having a hard time putting her language abilities to use. She initiated no conversation and her response to questions or directions was usually "huh?" When I taught in the resource room, children like Brooke were referred for testing for learning disabilities and usually came to me. I decided instead to keep Brooke in my classroom, but I had a reading tutor who worked with her and three other children for half an hour of our reading workshop time. The group read with the tutor in the same manner that the other children read with me, choosing their books or doing shared reading. She worked with only a few children, however, so that each one was allowed more "time on the air."

Brooke came to first grade with writing experience in kindergarten, but that was exclusively drawing. Writing was a choice activity in kindergarten, encouraged but not required. Brooke went to the writing center because she

Figure 11–1

One of Brooke's early drawings. "Erin is going to the pond."

liked to draw. When asked to talk about her drawings, she usually shrugged her shoulders, a habit she carried with her to first grade.

Brooke eagerly drew during our writing time. When asked to write about her drawings, she acted very dependent, with lots of shrugging and thumbsucking. The other four children who sat with Brooke were helpful. If she told me what her drawing was about, they would offer help with some of the sounds and letters (see Figure 11–1). Brooke had a few letter/sound associations of her own, but with their collaboration she began to put down writing. Recall of letter form was particularly hard for Brooke in the beginning of the year. By the end of the year she knew all forms, but had trouble making the distinction between some upper- and lowercase letters.

If writing was difficult for Brooke in the beginning, reading was impossible. Brooke liked books, and the better the illustrations, the more she liked them. But in terms of messages, meanings, and stories, she was cut off. If I asked Brooke what a book was about when she was looking at it, she would shrug. She did no retelling of stories, which is evidence of an in-head text and the kind of reading children do before they are able to attend to print. Another behavior that Brooke developed was throwing up her hands and saying, "I don't know." (I was glad because at least she was saying something!) Although she had some trouble attending to stories, Brooke enjoyed being read to. She would often sign out books that I read to the group in order to take them home and have them reread to her by her parents. Brooke wanted and needed to hear the stories again.

By the end of October, when I published her cat book (Figure 11–2) and she shared it with the class, Brooke was developing an awareness of print. She read and reread her book, looking at the pictures and trying to find the words. A month later Brooke wrote a sign book (Figure 11–3). We had worked on environmental print as a group in September and, as with all featured units of study, continued to refer to it. Brooke wrote her book at the time we were talking about smoking in our health unit.

By December, Brooke was truly interested in reading. She read an alphabet book with her friend Rachel during the large-group reading share time. Rachel read her half and cued Brooke on most of hers, but in a true spirit of collaboration. For the first time, Brooke shared a book by a professional writer. When she read her next book to the class, *Farm Counting Book* by Jane Miller, she did the reading by herself and was celebrated by her classmates. Around the same time she transcribed a favorite predictable story about three ducks. This was evidence of an interest in mastery of a particular book and of an in-head text.

Marshall, a friend of Brooke's, had written to Santa that he wanted a copy of *It Didn't Frighten Me* for Christmas. Since I know the author, I forwarded Marshall's letter. When he received the book in January, Marshall was so proud he stood up on his desk and read it to the class. Obviously impressed, Brooke quickly got the classroom copy, and two days later she shared it with the class. She delivered her reading with less gusto but with no less pride. She had to concentrate hard on the print; she also did much switching back and forth between art and print. This behavior became characteristic of her reading performances.

Figure 11–2

Brooke's cat book.

The Cat Book

by
Brooke Hodgdon

1

The cat with her baby.

2

And a yellow cat came.
He is the father cat.

3

And the father is scared
of ghosts on Halloween.

4

The cats are scared.

5

6

I am going to see a cat.

7

And I am tired today
and my cat is too.

8

I am coming to play
with my cat.

9

Figure 11–3

Brooke's sign book. (1) "No smoking sign means no smoking." (2) "Stop sign means you have to stop your car." (3) "The hospital sign means the hospital is close." (4) "Keep out sign means keep out of the place." (5) "One way sign means you go one way." (6) "Poison sign means it's poisonous." (7) "Speed limit means how fast you go." (8) "You go as fast as the sign says."

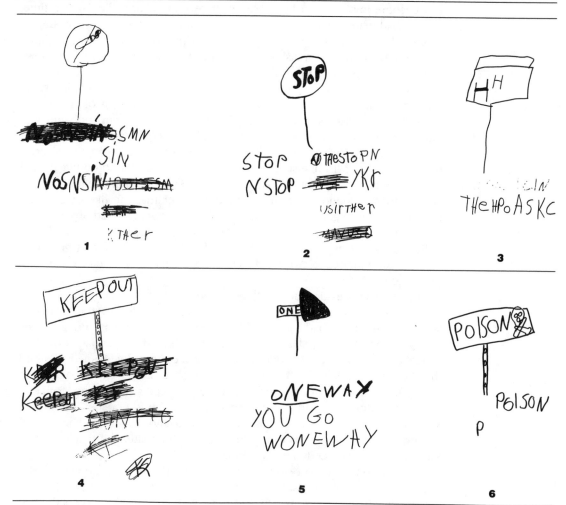

Print had begun to carry a lot of meaning for Brooke in both reading and writing. When she wrote her name book (Figure 11–4), she showed that words had become important to her because there was no drawing. By this time, Brooke had many demonstrations of reading and writing. She was talking to other children and me about her pieces. Drawing lost its significance, temporarily, but it had not been discouraged in any way. Her name book text shows her reliance on slotting to produce writing.

Brooke spent much of January and February at home because of illness, but she came back eager to read and write. She had a steady supply of predictable books from the classroom and reading lab. She also had writing tools and supplies available, and she made good use of all of the materials. When she returned to school, Brooke drafted her penpal letter (Figure 11–5) over a series of three days. Her list-like statements and questions are based on her penpal Kelley's letter. At one point, Brooke realized that she was asking Kelley what her favorite food was and Kelley had already told her that she liked pizza. She thought that this might be a problem and told me about it. I asked Brooke if she wanted to leave in her question or take it out. She decided to leave it in because Kelley might tell her other food that she liked. Kelley was a first grader in teacher-researcher Carol Avery's class in Pennsylvania, and we had a year-long exchange of letters.

Brooke's explanation of her illness came as a result of a conference with me just prior to writing the final copy. She brought her letter over and said that she was finished. She had had a conference with Rachel, who had no questions or suggestions. Since she had not put the letter in the finished basket but had brought the letter to me, I asked Brooke what she meant by finished. She said that she couldn't think of anything else to say. I asked Brooke if she thought that Kelley might be interested in the fact that she had been sick with mononucleosis and tonsillitis. She said yes but added that she could not spell the words. When I assured Brooke that she could write the sounds she heard, she was off. I rarely had to remind kids to use invented spelling after the first month of school, but Brooke needed the assurance.

Brooke continued to read predictable books throughout the winter. She brought a version of "The Ugly Duckling" to share with the group one day. She had gotten it from the reading lab, and although it is a simplification of the text with repetition, it has a narrative line. Brooke had practiced for days and gave a polished performance.

Brooke still used slotting in writing, but soon she began revision. In her "one" book (Figure 11–6), the tree page is a self-initiated revision. She also began using periods in her writing. When she brought her poem to group share, the children asked her a variety of questions, which resulted in Brooke's adding to her book. The questions (and her answers) were:

1. "Did you put a heart in the beginning and end on purpose?" "Yes." (This technique was later adopted by several classmates.)
2. "Why did you write this book?" "Because I like the number one."
3. "Are you going to do a two and a three book?" "I'll do up to four."
4. "There is only one sun. What else is there only one of?"

Figure 11–4
Brooke's name book. (1) "Rachel is my friend." (2) "Caleb is my cousin." (3) "Martha is my friend." (4) "Kara is my friend." (5) "Meghan is my friend." (6) "I like (Marshall) Marshall." (7) "My friend is Corinne." (8) "I like Glen Wood."

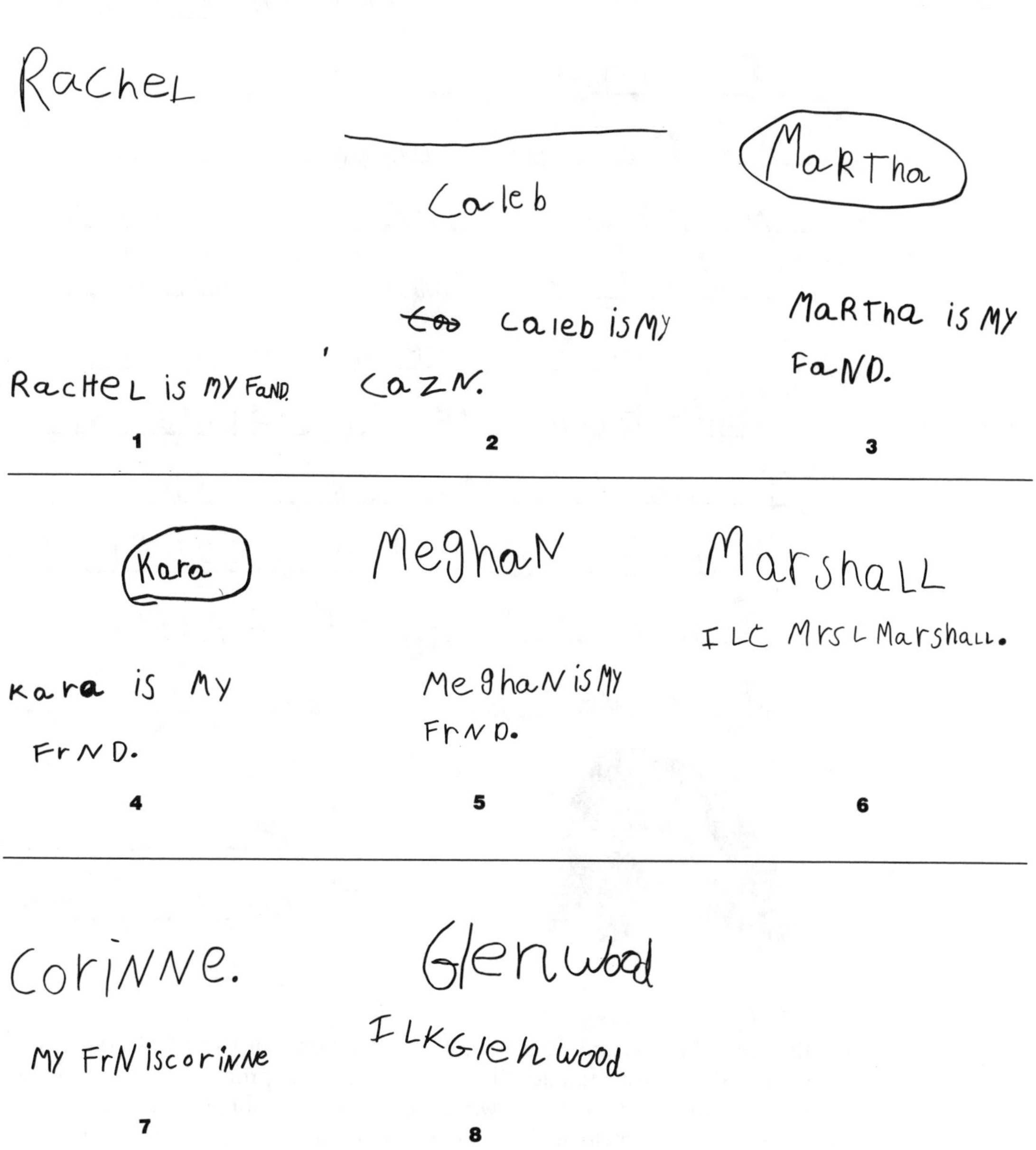

Rachel

_____

Caleb

(Martha)

Rachel is my Fand.

too Caleb is my
Cazn.

Martha is my
Fand.

1

2

3

(Kara)

Meghan

Marshall

I Lc Mrsl Marshall.

Kara is My
FrND.

Meghan is my
FrND.

4

5

6

CoriNNe.

My FrN is corinne

Glen wod

I LK Glen wood

7

8

Figure 11–5

Brooke's penpal letter.

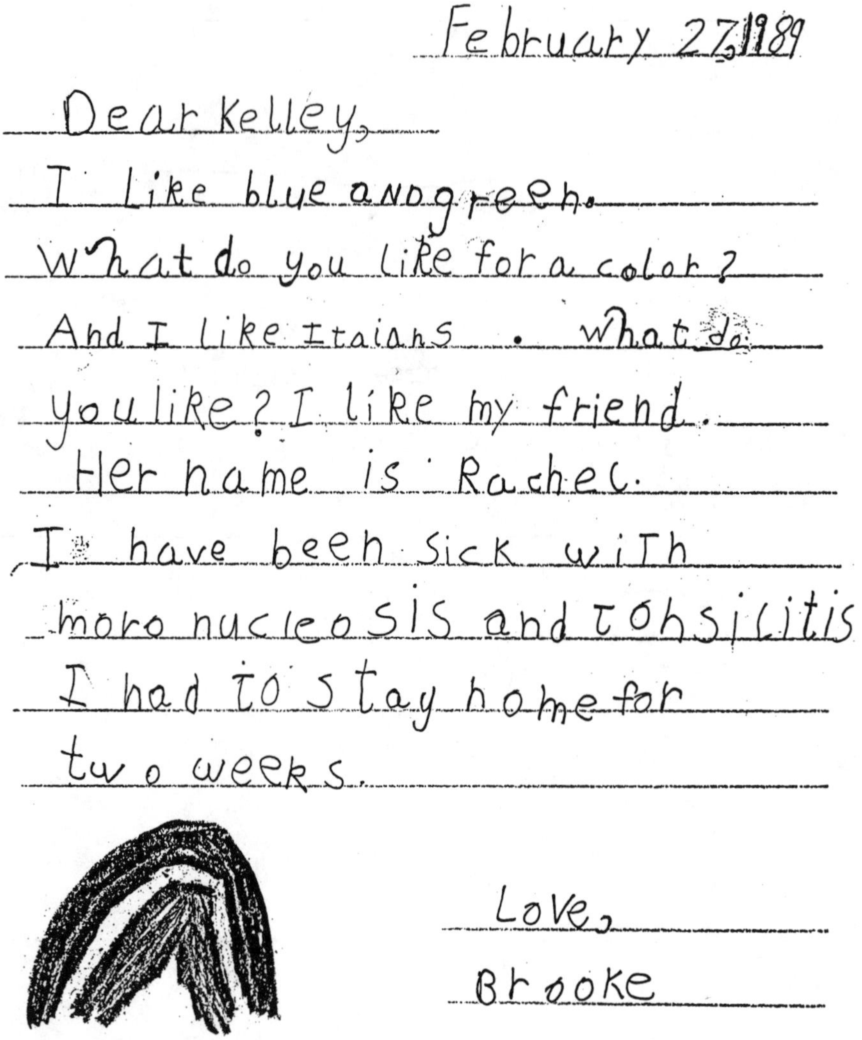

February 27,1989

Dear kelley,

I like blue and green.

What do you like for a color?

And I like Itaians . what do

you like? I like my friend.

Her name is Rachel.

I have been sick with

mono nucleosis and tohsicitis

I had to stay home for

two weeks.

Love,

Brooke

Brooke did not verbally answer the last question, but she added four pages (Figure 11–7) to the middle of her book. True to her promise, Brooke went on to a two book, but she didn't write about what was uniquely two. This time, however, Brooke included her first "about the author" page. Her name had just appeared in her friend Rachel's "about the author" page, providing a meaningful demonstration to her.

The next book she shared was a simple book called *The Easter Bunny's Lost Egg.* She continued with her intense concentration first on the picture and then on the print. Her one miscue was "box" for "basket," which she subsequently

Figure 11-6

Brooke's "one" book. (1) "There is one heart." (2) "And a tree and that is one tree." (3) "There is one one." (4) "And there is a bow." (5) "There is one question mark." (6) "There is one sun." (11) "There is one S." (12) "There is one red heart."

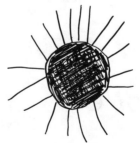

Tr is one HrAT

1

unD A Tree aND TAT is one Tree.

2

Tr is one ONE

3

and Tar is A BoW

4

There his one KACTAK

5

Tar is one SUN

6

Tus is one S

11

Ta is one raD HAit

12

Figure 11–7

Additions to Brooke's "one" book. (7) "There is only one moon." (8) "There is only one God." (9) "There is only one Jesus." (10) "I like the world, there is only one world.

Tar   is oLe oNe

mooh

7

Tar   is oLe oNe

G oD

8

Tar[s]oLeoNe
Jesus

9

I   LiKe
THe wrLD
Tar isoLe
oNe WrLD

10

self-corrected. It was evident from this performance and other readings that Brooke's sight vocabulary was growing.

In April, our school had a distribution of books through the federal program Reading is Fundamental. Brooke chose Cynthia Rylant's *When I Was Young in the Mountains,* probably because of the fine illustrations, by Diane Goode. Brooke read and reread her book through the illustrations and asked to have the story read to her over and over at school and at home. At that same time Brooke discovered *Little Bear,* and she read and reread that book for the words. She then went on to the other Little Bear books. Brooke was able to identify books as poetry, fiction, and nonfiction as her awareness of books grew. By spring she loved being read to.

Toward the end of the year, when Brooke wrote about her sisters (Figure 11–8), there was finally a trace of a narrative line. Brooke had begun to read stories so she began to write them as well. She also revised her story after sharing it with the class. The italics show the additions that Brooke made to expand and clarify her writing according to her readers' needs. When Brooke came back from a weekend in early June, she told me that she was writing a book about her family at home, and she brought it to school to show me. Writing and reading for Brooke were genuine activities.

Consistently, Brooke's writing reflected her reading and her reading mirrored her writing. Art had always been important; words and print developed importance. Talk surrounded both, and Brooke was able to take an active part in that talk. She considered herself a reader and a writer, and she was part of our social and literary community.

Gregory

Gregory's mother called school in early August and asked me to return her call. I did so, and a child answered. When I asked to speak to his mother, he told me, "Her can't come. Her busy." Hearing a baby crying in the background, I told the child who I was and said I would call back another time. In a few minutes, Gregory's mother returned my call. At first I was surprised, thinking that I had given my message to a preschool child. Then I realized that I had been talking to six-year-old Gregory, who was not as young as he sounded. He could relay a meaningful message.

Gregory's kindergarten teacher had recommended that he repeat kindergarten because he was immature. Gregory was young; he had just turned six at the time I met with his mother in August, but his language delay made him appear much younger. Besides, Gregory loved to play and sitting made him fidget. A small and very lean boy with bright blue eyes, Gregory was constantly in motion. He loved to explore, invent, and take things apart.

During our meeting, Gregory's mother told me that he had been in kindergarten in Florida for the first half of his kindergarten year. There he was enrolled in language therapy and appeared to be making progress. When they moved to Maine, the language therapy was not continued, and she felt that he did not do very well in school generally. She decided against the recommenda-

Figure 11–8

Brooke's book about her sisters. (1) "I am playing with my sisters. My sisters (are) names are Erin and Kacey." (2) "We are playing ball." (3) *It is time to for my sisters to go to bed. It is 6:00.* (4) *"I am watching T.V."*

I aM playing
with My ~~saStro~~
SaStrDrs
My SaStrS
Are NaMSAre
ErIN AND kacEy

1

we Are pLaying
~~Blu~~

2

~~ITIS TIM TO GO~~
~~To Bad~~
For My ~~ITIS TIM~~
Nas ToGo
ToBaD
At is 6:00

3

I ~~AM~~ wush
~~Tev~~ TV

4

Figure 11-8

(5) "Now it is time for me to go to bed." (6) "My Mom is tucking me into bed *at 7:00.*" (7) *"The next day* I am playing with one of my sisters." (8) "The end."

Naw it is tom
For Me To GoTo Bad

5

My MoM is
Taking Me
in To Bad
AT 7:00

6

the naxt Day
I'm paeing
with ~~My~~ one
of My sastrs

7

The END

8

tion for retention because she felt that she had not been involved enough with Gregory's schooling. I wondered about Gregory's language development and recommended that we have him tested when school began.

Even without testing it was obvious that Gregory was bright but his language was delayed. On one test, he scored at the fifth percentile in sentence imitation, or like a three-year-old. His high score was at the eighty-fourth percentile, or as nearly an eight-year-old (7–9), in grammatical understanding. This, of course, was only one piece of information about Gregory's language, but it showed that there was a marked distinction between his overall speaking score and his overall listening score. Even though there was a lot of time devoted to speaking and listening in the classroom, and I wanted him there as much as possible, I agreed with the recommendation for an hour of language therapy a week because of Gregory's scrambled syntax, unclear expression due to articulation problems, and his mother's high anxiety.

Gregory's reading had a slow start. He had been read to. He had favorite books that he brought into class the first week of school. He was interested in, but not overly conscious of, environmental print, which I featured at the beginning of the year. He could not recite or read a nursery rhyme. Predictable books that utilize rhyme and rhythm were a mystery to Gregory, as were all the books based on songs that we read together. But Gregory wanted to take part, and he did, trying to catch a word here and there in a group reading.

Illustrations in books meant more to Gregory than the print did at first. When I featured alphabet books and counting books, he began to get interested in reading. Reading his first published book, "Ghosts," also contributed to his awareness of print and growing interest in reading. Furthermore, many of Gregory's classmates had begun to read formally and shared their reading with the class.

After Christmas vacation, Gregory's mother called to report her excitement as Gregory started noticing rhyme and reading environmental print in the grocery store. She had been reading to him continually, and now he began to read to her. (He was one of the most active children in our home/school reading program, due to his mother's commitment.) Gregory was able to rely on familiar story structures and responded well to our shared readings of folk tales and fairy tales. He was able to do skeletal retellings, or in-head texts, of books. His sense of story and awareness of literary language were well developed because he had been read to. Around this time Gregory developed a number of sight words, which allowed him to enter unfamiliar books.

Like Brooke, Gregory responded strongly to the art in books, even as his awareness of printed text grew. During read-aloud sessions, Gregory was often restless, but the illustrations always caught his eye. When he chose books, it was often because of the illustrations. One of his favorites was *Need a House? Call Ms. Mouse!,* by George Mendoza. I featured it in the fall when I read a series of house books, and Gregory read it throughout the year.

During our shared reading of *Little Bear* in February, Gregory enjoyed the stories and the character of Little Bear very much. Earlier, during the fall and early winter, it had been hard for him to sustain his attention to print/art/text. But by late winter he was rapt. His legs scissored ninety mph, but his eyes and brain were right with the author. Gregory had difficulty with his part in our choral reading of "The Owl and the Pussycat," which we did a few weeks later, but he held his own with his partner.

Before Easter, Gregory brought in a tape and book of Peter Cottontail. He was reading and singing the song and had copies made for everyone in the class. When Gregory picked up and read *The Lady with the Alligator Purse* a few days later, I smiled and thought of the days when not even *I Know an Old Lady* read with the group meant much to him.

During the spring, Gregory began to read books in series: the Frog and Toad books, by Arnold Lobel; the Clifford books, by Norman Bridwell; the Arthur series, by Marc Brown; and Peggy Parish's Amelia Bedelia books. He wrote about his books in a journal with Marshall. His letters to Marshall, one of which is shown in Figure 11–9, were basically lists of what he read and liked, but he was learning to use a journal in reading. Occasionally, he posed questions in his journal like this one: "Amelia Bedelia. Is she a woman or a girl?"

At the beginning of the year, writing seemed more like something Gregory could do than reading. The first time he recorded what he told me in response to my question about his drawing (Figure 11–10), we counted the words in his sentence, and I drew six lines on his paper because he did not know how his words went down on paper. Since he had choice whether or not to write in kindergarten, I suspected that he had done so infrequently. Gregory knew most of his letter/sound associations, so he could use invented spelling fairly efficiently.

Figure 11–9

One of Gregory's letters to Marshall. "Dear Marshall and Mrs. Stires, I like to read and I like to read *Ox Cart Man* by Donald Hall and I like to read *Katy [and the Big Snow]* and I like to read *Mike Mulligan and His Steamshovel.* Love Gregory."

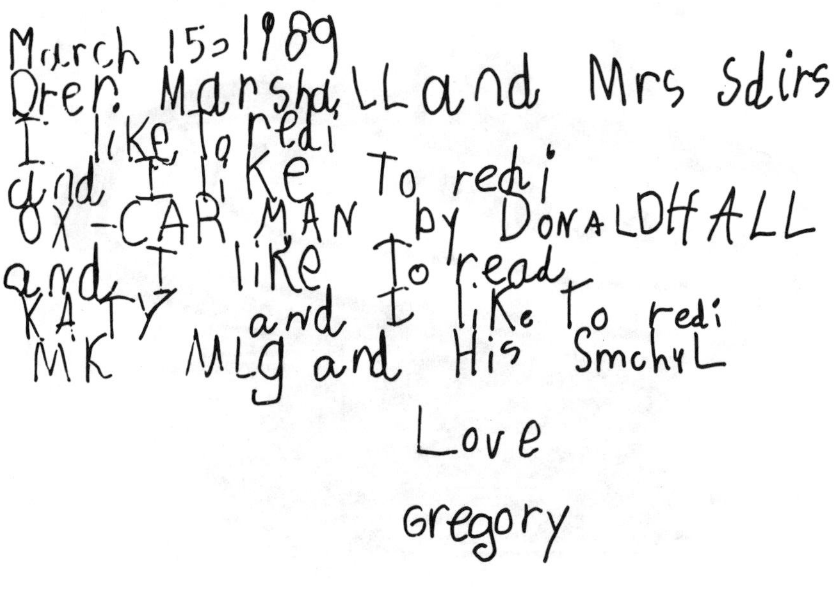
March 15, 1989
Drer Marshall and Mrs Sdirs
I like to redi
and I like To redi
OX-CAR MAN by DONALDHALL
and I like To read
KATY and I like To redi
MK MLG and His SmchyL
Love
Gregory

In September, Gregory fluctuated between labels, expanded labels, and simple sentences in his journal writing. If I asked him about a label and picture, he could tell me more. It wasn't always possible to understand his elaborations, but I encouraged him to add to his text. He sometimes did so if I was with him. A month later, Gregory could sustain a personal narrative in book form (Figure 11–11). Although Gregory explained that his day at his father's work had ended after lunch, I wondered if he had run out of steam or out of pages. At the parent conference, Gregory's father was delighted with the story and confirmed Gregory's explanation.

In November, Gregory built upon his narrative frame and wrote an imaginary story. He did not illustrate. He wrote:

One day, a rainy day and it stopped and my dad was happy and my mom was happy, too. And a rainbow stayed out and we went to the hill. And [when] we were having breakfast and then I went out the doors and I played by the rainbow. And then I climbed up the

---

Figure 11–10
One of Gregory's early drawings. "The submarine is in the water."

Figure 11–11

Gregory's first book, "My Work." (1) "We ride the van to my work." (2) "I am in my work." (3) "This is my chairs." (4) "I am sitting in my chair." (5) "I am starting to have my lunch." (6) "I am eating." (7) "Now I am going home."

rainbow and then I was up the rainbow. Then I had my lunch and I worked and build a rainbow house. Then I was finished and I played in my rainbow house.

Gregory did not give up on illustrating, but it no longer held the meaning of the text; the words did. In his next narrative, about going to Jacob's birthday party (Figure 11–12), Gregory wrote quickly using mainly initial and final consonants with a few experimental vowels. Although I encouraged Gregory to write all of the sounds he could hear, I did not require him to do so. I was more interested in Gregory's working with language than sounds. Gregory also did a lot of talking about his texts and other subjects during writing. I encouraged that.

   Gregory's penpal in Carol Avery's class, who was also named Gregory, had remarkably similar handwriting. In his letter (Figure 11–13), Gregory doesn't respond to anything in the other Gregory's letter, but he does include questions the way his penpal did. His letter is a list of likes. This genre was important for Gregory because it helped him to develop a sense of audience.

Figure 11–12

Gregory's birthday party narrative. "I said to Jacob, Happy birthday to you, happy birthday, dear Jacob."

Gregory often did things that gave me pause. He loved shorthand. He consistently used "n" for "and" long after the conventional spelling had been taught in a minilesson and in a conference with him. When I asked him why he kept using "n" for "and," he said, "Oh, it's just quicker." The next day he came over to show me his conventional spelling. One day in February, Gregory stapled the first and last page of his blank drafting booklet to the covers. When I asked him why he did that, he went to the bookshelf and got a book with particularly nice endpapers and said he was making his book like that. I told the class about endpapers in a minilesson.

Figure 11–13

Gregory's penpal letter.

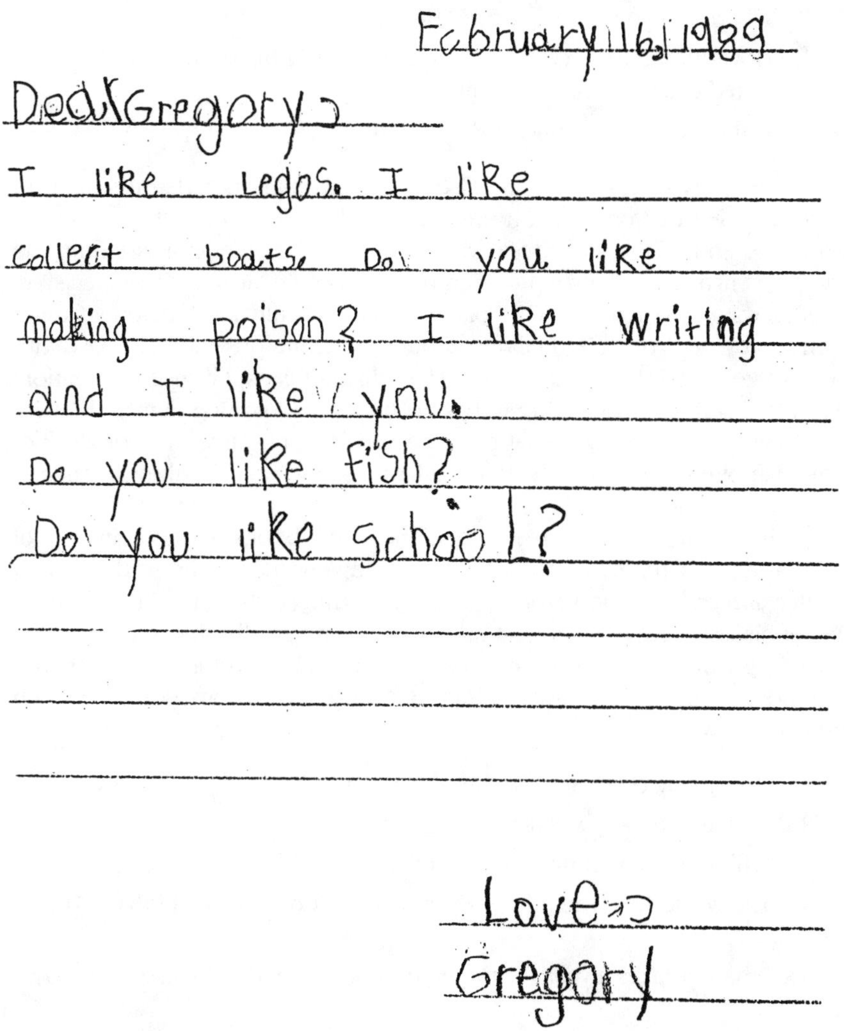

February 16, 1989

Dear Gregory,

I like Legos. I like collect boats. Do you like making poison? I like writing and I like you.

Do you like fish?

Do you like school?

Love,
Gregory

Gregory also did minilessons. In the beginning of his story "The Fish Dies" Gregory used dialogue to help tell the story, and he experimented with quotation marks. I knew that this was a demonstration that Gregory picked up on in his reading. I collaborated with him so that the use of the marks was clear to the other first graders. The next day, when Gregory finished his brief story and brought it to group share, his classmates were concerned with content. He had written:

> "Let's go to the fish," said P.J.
> "Okay," said Gregory.
> And the fish was dead, but when
> they went back, the fish was alive.
> And then they were happy,
> The end.

They asked and he answered:

1. "Where did you see the fish?" "In the water."
2. "How did the fish get alive?" "He had a cut in his stomach and he looked dead, but he came alive."
3. "Is this fiction or nonfiction?" "It is true."

The discussion was lively, and Gregory filled us in on parts missing from the text. He left us wondering, however, when he said that the story was true, and at the end of the share, one child remarked, "Something is telling me that this is fiction." The group conference did not result in a single revision. Revision was yet to come for Gregory, who had difficulty focusing on anything but the present. Writing and talking about the writing provided Gregory with a way to go back over his language, revisualizing his experience or creation. Clarity was still the major issue in both speaking and writing during the winter. Gregory didn't realize what parts he had left out, mixed up, or did not name. He often filled in with "that stuff, you know" or "the thing I can not know."

In the spring, when we researched and wrote books on the countries of South America, Gregory learned to pronounce Venezuela as he studied about it with a fifth-grade collaborator. He enjoyed learning facts and writing a report. One of his last pieces was nonfiction, and it was no small subject. It was titled "About the World," and it is reproduced in Figure 11–14. After Gregory shared with the large group, they asked him the following questions, some of which resulted in revisions:

1. "How many countries are there?" "Ninety-nine."
2. "How do you know that?" "I just think so."
3. "Where could you find out?" "In the library."
4. "The world has sand and grass and water. Could you add that?" "I guess so."
5. "I think it takes a year for the earth to go around the sun. Could you add that?"

Figure 11–14

Gregory's book "About the World." (1) "The world moves very slow." (2) "And there are *170* countries in the world." (3) "The world is a big world." (4) "The world moves around the sun in a circle in _____." (5) "People go around the world in a spaceship." (6) The world is filled with dirt *and sand and grass and water and trees.*" (7) "There are foxes and rabbits and deer and other animals."

The woard mvsa vore SlOW.

1

and Thir are 170 ~~oz~~ counTRes in the woard.

2

The woard is a Big woad.

3

The woardlmuvs aread the suniia eira in ____

4

Pelple go arand The woard With a sbishp.

5

The woard is fld With drtx and sad and gras and water a trees.

6

thir are fixse and rabbit and ~~drseg~~ and athir anmos.

7

Gregory's additions went beyond the questions of the group and showed that he was revisualizing, that he knew that he had more to say to his readers/listeners. The writing and talking about writing (and he probably did more talking about writing than actual writing in the spring) was paying off. At the same time Gregory's oral language was changing. He was self-correcting and pausing to think through before responding orally. Gregory worked at making himself clear to an audience.

I believe that Brooke and Gregory grew steadily as readers and writers because the conditions for language and literacy were present in our classroom. Early in my teaching career I realized that some children, even in poor learning environments, learned in spite of their teachers and those environments, but other children certainly did not. Later, when I was a resource room teacher, I saw that some children did not learn in healthy environments with devoted teachers. What I hoped to do was to provide an environment where all my children could learn. Tracing Gregory's and Brooke's progress convinces me that they did learn, without being labeled and sent out of the classroom for long periods of time each day. They could and did learn in the classroom with their classmates.

References

Bonne, Rose. 1961. *I Know an Old Lady.* Illustrated by Abner Graboff. New York: Scholastic.

Cambourne, Brian. 1987. "Language, Learning and Literacy." In *Towards a Reading-Writing Classroom,* edited by Andrea Butler and Jan Turbill. Portsmouth, NH: Heinemann.

Goss, Janet L., and Jerome C. Harste. 1981. *It Didn't Frighten Me.* Illustrated by Steve Romney. School Book Fairs.

Gordon, Sharon. 1980. *Easter Bunny's Lost Egg.* Illustrated by John Magine. Mahwah, NJ: Troll Associates.

Heath, Shirley Brice. 1983. *Ways with Words: Language, Life, and Work in Communities and Classrooms.* New York: Cambridge University Press.

Mendoza, George. 1981. *Need a House? Call Ms. Mouse!* Illustrated by Doris Susan Smith. New York: Grosset and Dunlap.

Miller, Jane. 1983. *Farm Counting Book.* New York: Prentice-Hall.

Minarik, Else Holmelund. 1957. *Little Bear.* Illustrated by Maurice Sendak. New York: Scholastic.

Rylant, Cynthia. 1982. *When I Was Young in the Mountains.* Illustrated by Diane Goode. New York: E.P. Dutton.

Stires, Susan. 1988. "Reading and Talking: 'Special' Readers Show They Know." In *Understanding Writing,* edited by Thomas Newkirk and Nancie Atwell. Portsmouth, NH: Heinemann.

Wells, Gordon. 1986. *The Meaning Makers: Children Learning Language and Using Language to Learn.* Portsmouth, NH: Heinemann.

Westcott, Nadine Bernard. 1988. *The Lady with the Alligator Purse.* Boston: Little, Brown.

III. Reasons, Visions, and Reflections

12. All Children Can Write

Donald H. Graves

I stood at the side of Ms. Richards's third-grade classroom watching the children write. We were at the beginning of our two-year National Institute of Education study of children's composing processes. The school had diagnosed two of the children in Ms. Richards's room as having severe visual-motor problems. They were not hard to find.

Both leaned over their papers, their elbows crooked at right angles to their bodies to protect the appearance of their papers. I walked over to take a closer look at one of the two children's papers. Billy's paper was smudged, wrinkled, letters blackened; in several instances, his paper was thinned and blackened still more where he had gone through several spelling trials on the same word. The more serious aspect of Billy's writing profile was not his visual-motor difficulty, the appearance of his paper, or his numerous misspellings. Billy was a self-diagnosed poor writer. He connected his writing problems with a lack of worthwhile ideas and experiences. In addition, he was well versed in what he couldn't do.

Billy had been in a separate program emphasizing visual-motor skills, letter formation, and various fine-motor tasks. No question, using a pencil was painful and arduous for him. Teachers complained that Billy rarely completed his work and was constantly behind the others, though he seemed to be articulate. Billy's program was skill-based, disconnected from meaning, and filled with positive reinforcement about his ability to form letters on good days. There was no attempt to connect his writing with the communication of ideas.

Children with learning disabilities often work on skills in isolation, disconnected from learning itself, and therefore disconnected from themselves as persons. Therefore, like Billy, though their skills may improve slightly in isolation, the children do not perceive the function of the skill. Worse, they do not see the skill as a means to show what they know. Skills-work merely supplies additional evidence for the misconception that they are less intelligent than other children.

Billy was in a classroom that stressed writing as a process. This meant the children received help from the time they chose a topic to the time they completed their final work. Ms. Richards played the believing game, starting with what Billy knew, particularly his experiences. In fact, Billy's breakthrough as a writer came when his teacher discovered his interest in and knowledge of gardening. As Ms. Richards helped him to teach her about this subject, she learned how to plant, cultivate, water, fertilize, and provide special care for certain varieties of tomatoes. Although Billy wrote more slowly than the other children, he became lost in his subject, forgot about his poor spelling and handwriting, ceased to cover his paper, and wrote a piece filled with solid information about gardening. Once Billy connected writing with knowing—his knowing—it was then possible to work with his visual-motor and spelling problems, but as incidental to communicating information.

Ms. Richards is now one of the thousands of teachers in the United States and the English-speaking world who teach writing as a process. New research and publications, university courses, and numerous summer institutes are now helping teachers and administrators to find out for themselves what students can do when they focus on the meaning of their writing. Much of the focus of these institutes and courses is on the teachers' own writings: most of us had to rediscover the power of writing for ourselves before we could learn to hear what these young writers had to teach us.

Although writing-process work helps all writers, it seems to be particularly successful with people who see themselves as disenfranchised from literacy. I place in this group learners like Billy, who have diagnosed learning disabilities and the accompanying "I-don't-know-anything" syndrome.

The writing-process approach to teaching focuses on children's ideas and helps children teach the teacher or other children in the class what they know, with emphasis first given to ideas and clarifying. This is the first experience many children have with other humans who work hard to point to what they know, instead of what is lacking in the message. Small wonder then that the writing process works best with the disenfranchised, who become a bit giddy at the prospect of seeing their words on paper affecting the thinking of others.

Understanding writing as communication is the heart of teaching the writing process. This discussion will first focus on the nature of writing, look in greater detail at research on the writing process itself, examine two principles in teaching writing, and then describe four basics in establishing a writing program. It also has a brief section on further reading and recommendations for summer programs for people interested in continuing their study of the writing process.

What is writing?

Writing is a medium with which people communicate with themselves and with others at other places and times. When I write, I write to learn what I know because I don't know fully what I mean until I order the words on paper. Then I see ... and know. Writers' first attempts to make sense are crude, rough approximations of what they mean. Writing makes sense of things for oneself, then for others.

Children can share their writing with others by reading aloud, by chatting with friends while writing, or (in more permanent form) by publishing. Billy found that writing carried a different authority from spoken words. When he took the gardening piece out in December, he found that words written in September could be savored three months later. Furthermore, when he read the published books of other children in his classroom, he began to realize that his book on gardening was read by others when he wasn't present.

Written language is different from oral language. When Billy speaks, he reinforces his meaning by repeating words and phrases. Unlike when he writes, an audience is present; when the audience wanders or indicates disagreement, he changes his message with words, hand signals, facial expressions, and body posture. This is the luxury of oral discourse. "Error," adjustment, and experimentation are an expected part of oral discourse.

There is a different tradition surrounding most teaching of writing. Only one attempt, one draft, is allowed to communicate full meaning (without an audience response). Red-lined first drafts are the norm; we blanche at any misspellings or crudely formed letters.

Still worse, writing has been used as a form of punishment: "Write your misspelled word twenty-five times" (this is called reinforcement of visual-memory systems); "Write one hundred times, 'I will not chew gum in school' "; "Write a 300-word composition on how you will improve your attitude toward school." Most teachers teaching in 1985 were bathed in the punishment syndrome when they were learning to write. Small wonder that most of us subtly communicate writing as a form of punishment. We have known no other model of teaching.

The writing process

When children use a meaning-centered approach to writing, they compose in idiosyncratic ways. Each child's approach to composing is different from the next's. Some draw first, write two words, and in ten minutes or less announce, "I'm done." Others draw after writing or do not write at all; instead, they speak with a neighbor about what they will write. Some stare out the window or at the blank page and write slowly after twenty minutes of reflection. At some point in their development, writers believe one picture and two words beneath the drawing contain an entire story. In the writer's mind, the story is complete; members of the audience shake their heads and try to work from drawing to text and back to understand the author's intent.

Such idiosyncratic approaches by children seem capricious to outsiders, confusing to children, and bewildering to us as teachers. We intervene with story starters to "get them going," produce pictures as stimuli for writing, and consult language arts texts for language activities. The texts provide "systematic" approaches, often through the teaching of the sentence, then two sentences, and finally development of the paragraph. Our detailed observation of young children writing shows they simply don't learn that way. Rather, they write three sentences in one in their first year, not understanding where one sentence ends and the other begins. Studies of children's understanding and use of sentences show they don't acquire full sentence sense until much later (about fifth grade).

The most pernicious aspect of teacher interventions is that children begin to learn early on that others need to supply topics because they come to the page with nothing in their heads. A focus on skills and form to the exclusion of child-initiated meaning further confirms their lack of fit with the writing process.

Prepared materials seek to reduce the stress and the uncertainty that writers face when they encounter the blank page. But the attempt to produce certainty through standardization bypasses the opportunity for child growth. There is good reason to expect tension when a child first writes.

When writers write, they face themselves on the blank page. That clean white piece of paper is like a mirror. When I put words on the page, I construct an image of myself on that whiteness. I may not like my spelling, handwriting, choice of words, aesthetics, or the general cleanliness of the page. Until I can begin to capture what I want to say, I have to be willing to accept imperfection and ambiguity. If I arrive at the blank page with a writing history filled with problems, I am already predisposed to run from what I see. I try to hide my paper, throw it away, or mumble to myself, "This is stupid." But with every dangerous, demanding situation, there is an opportunity to learn. Teachers who follow and accompany children as they compose help them to deal with what they see on the page. The reason writing helps children with learning disabilities is that they do far more than learn to write: They learn to come to terms with a new image of themselves as thinkers—thinkers with a message to convey to the world.

Teaching writing—two basic principles

After twelve years of working with writing research and the teaching of writing, I have found two principles essential for effective teaching of writing: (1) The teacher teaches most by showing how he/she learns, and (2) the teacher provides a highly structured classroom.

The best demonstration of how teachers learn is through their gathering of information from the children. They place the children in the position of teaching them what they know, usually through conferences. "Now you say that you have to be careful how deep you plant lettuce, Billy. Can you tell me more about that? And do you think the precise depth should be in your piece for the other children? Will they want to know that?" Billy's teacher has shown him how she learns and how he should learn to listen to questions he soon will be able to ask himself.

Ms. Richards, Billy's teacher, has a basic life-style of learning from everyone. Whether seated next to someone on a plane, in the teachers' room, or talking informally with children, she wants to be taught; in a lifetime she has learned how important it is to help others to teach her. People leave Ms. Richards surprised they knew so much about their subjects.

Ms. Richards's classroom is a highly structured, predictable classroom. Children who learn to exercise choice and responsibility can function only in a structured room. Furthermore, the up-and-down nature of the writing process itself demands a carefully defined room. Predictability means that writing occurs daily, at set times, with the teacher moving in the midst of the children, listening to their intentions, worries, and concerns. They know she will be nearby attending to their work. She rarely addresses the entire class during writing time. She works hard to establish a studio atmosphere. Predictability also means she won't solve problems for them. Rather, she asks how they might approach the problem. She listens, clarifies their intentions and their problems, and moves on.

Children learn to take responsibility not only for their topics, content of their drafts, and final copy, but also for carrying out classroom decisions. A structured classroom requires an organized teacher who has set the room up to run itself. The teacher has already made a list of the things to be done to help the room function. From September through June, he or she gradually passes on those duties to the children. Attendance, caring for room plants and animals, room cleanliness, lunch lines, desk supervision, and cleaning are but a few examples of these delegations. When room structure and routine do not function well, the teacher and students plan together for the best way to make it function more smoothly. Ms. Richards's room is based on extensive preparation in room design and knowledge of materials, the children, and the process by which they learn to take responsibility.

Teachers who function well in teaching the writing process are interested in what children have to teach them. Writing-process teaching is responsive, demanding teaching that helps children solve problems in the writing process and in the classroom.

Carrying out a writing-process program

I am often asked, "What are the essentials to strong writing programs?" Although the list could be extensive, I think that if teachers understand the following four components, their writing programs will serve the children well. These components are (1) adequate provision of time, (2) child choice of topic, (3) responsive teaching, and (4) the establishment of a classroom community, a community that has learned to help itself.

Time.   Our data show that children need to write a minimum of four days a week to see any appreciable change in the quality of their writing. It takes that amount of writing to contribute to their personal development as learners. Unless children write at least four days a week, they won't like it. Once-a-week writing (the national average is about one day in eight) merely reminds them they can't write; they never write often enough to listen to their writing. Worse, the teacher simply has no access to the children. He or she has to scurry madly around the room trying to reach each child. With little access to the children, the teacher can't help them take responsibility, solve problems for themselves, or listen to their responses and questions. The very important connection between speaking and writing is lost.

Although teaching writing four to five times a week helps the teacher, it helps the children even more. When children write on a daily basis, we find they write when they aren't writing. Children get into their subjects, thinking about their texts and topics when they are riding on buses, lying in bed, watching television, reading books, or taking trips. When they write regularly, papers accumulate. There is visible evidence they know and are growing. They gain experience in choosing topics and very soon have more topics to write about than class time can accommodate. Children with learning problems need even more time. They need to learn to listen to themselves with help from the teacher. In summary, regular writing helps:

1. Children choose topics.
2. Children listen to their pieces and revise.
3. Children help each other.
4. Teachers listen to child texts.
5. Skills develop in the context of child pieces.
6. Teachers to have greater access to children.

Topic choice.   The most important thing children can learn is what they know and how they know it. Topic choice, a subject the child is aware that he knows something about, is at the heart of success in writing. Billy struggled with handwriting and spelling and equated those problems with not knowing topics to write about. When his teacher helped him to discover his knowledge and interest in gardening, he began to write, first haltingly, then with greater flow. Billy was open to help with spelling and handwriting when he knew he had something to say. Skills are important; learning disabilities cannot be ignored, but neither can teachers or researchers forget that writing exists to communicate with self and others.

"How can I get the child to write? Do you have any good motivators?" are frequent questions asked of me in workshops. The word *get* embraces the problem. There are thousands of "motivators" on the market in the form of story starters, paragraph starters, computer software, animated figures, picture starters, and exciting "sure-fire" interest getters. We forget that children are very sophisticated consumers of motivators from Saturday morning television alone. Worse, motivators teach the child that the best stimulus comes from the outside. Writing actually demands dozens of motivators during the course of composing, but they are motivators that can only be supplied by the writer himself. All children have important experiences and interests they can learn to tap through writing. If children are to become independent learners, we have to help them know what they know; this process begins with helping children to choose their own topics.

Very young children, ages five through seven, have very little difficulty choosing topics, especially if they write every day. As children grow older and experience the early effects of audience, even under favorable learning conditions, they begin to doubt what they know. From that point on, all writers go through a kind of doubting game about the texts they produce. They learn to read better and are more aware of the discrepancy between their texts and their actual intentions. If, however, overly severe, doubting teachers are added to the internal doubts of the child, writing becomes still more difficult.

If children write every day and share their writing, we find they use each other as the chief stimulus for topic selection. If teachers write with their children, demonstrating the origin of their topics, and surround the children with literature, topic selection is even easier.

Topic selection is helped through daily journal writing, where children take ten minutes to record their thoughts. Teachers may also give five- to ten-minute writing assignments, such as: "Write about how you think our room could be improved" (just following a discussion about how the room could be improved with the entire class) or "That upsets you? Well, blast away on paper with the first thoughts that come to mind. But write it for you; if you feel like showing it to me, okay." The teacher finds many occasions where it is useful to record thoughts and opinions on paper. Each of these approaches demonstrates what writing is for, as well as helping the children to have access to what they know and think.

Response.   People write to share, whether with themselves or others. Writers need audiences to respond to their messages. The response confirms for the writer that the text fits her intentions. First, the teacher provides an active audience for the writer by confirming what she understands in the text and then by asking a few clarifying questions. Second, the teacher helps the entire class to learn the same procedure during group share time. Each writing period ends with two or three children sharing their pieces with the group while the group follows the discipline of first pointing to what is in the text, then asking questions to learn more about the author's subject. All of these responses, whether by the teacher or the other children, are geared to help writers learn to listen to their own texts.

While the children are writing, Billy's teacher moves around the room, responding to their work in progress. Here is an interchange Ms. Richards had with Billy about his piece "My Garden," the text of which is presented below:

MY GRDAN
I help my Dad with the grdan ferstyou have to dig it up an than you rake an get the racks out of it. Than you make ros an you haveto be cerfull to make it deep enuff so the letis will come up.

Ms. Richards first receives the piece by saying what she understands about what Billy has written:

Ms. Richards: You've been working hard, Billy. I see that you work with your dad on your garden. You know just what you do; you dig it up, rake it to get the rocks out, and then you have to be careful how deep you plant things. Did I get that right?

Billy: Yup.

Ms. Richards: Well, I was wondering, Billy. You say that the lettuce has to be planted deep enough so the lettuce will come up. Could you tell me more about that? I haven't planted a garden for a long time.

Billy: Well, if you plant it too deep, it won't come up. Lettuce is just near the top.

Ms. Richards: Oh, I see, and did you plant some other things in your garden?

Billy: Yup, carrots, beans, turnips (I hate 'em), spinach (that, too), beets, and tomatoes; I like tomatoes.

Ms. Richards: That's quite a garden, Billy. And what will you be writing here next?

Billy: You have to water it once you plant it.

Ms. Richards: Then you already know what you'll be doing, don't you.

There are many problems with Billy's text: misspelled words, run-on sentences, missing capitalizations, and incomplete information. But Billy has just started writing his piece. Therefore, Ms. Richards works on word flow, helping Billy to know that he knows something about his subject and that he has a clear understanding of what he will do next. Later, when his piece is finished, she will choose one skill to teach within the context of his topic. Above all, she works hard to help Billy teach her about his subject, to keep control of the topic in his hands, no matter how uncertain Billy might feel about his subject.

Notice that Ms. Richards has spent no more than a minute and a half in response. She then moves to other children while responding in the same manner, receiving a text and asking questions. As she moves to different children in other parts of the room (she does not move in rotation or down rows; the movement appears to be random), the other children can hear that the teacher expects them to help her with what they know. Lengthy responses tend to take the writing away from the child. For example, if Ms. Richards were to say, "I had a garden once, Billy. I planted all kinds of things too: I planted cabbages, those same turnips, yellow beans, pole beans, and corn. Yes, it's hard work," she'd be identifying with Billy's garden and the hard work that goes into it, but *she* is now the informant. Such sharing should come only when his piece is completed and his authorship of this piece established.

Ms. Richards's statement is specific. When she receives Billy's text, she uses the actual words he has composed on the page. All writers need to know their words (the actual words on the page) affect other people. Notice that very little praise is given to Billy in this type of response. Instead, the listener, Ms. Richards, points with interest to the words; they are strong enough for her to understand and to remember them. The use of specifics, rather than the exclusive use of praise, is a fundamental issue in helping Billy to maintain control of his piece, as well as to take more responsibility for his text.

Establish a community of learners.   Writing is a social act. If social actions are to work, then the establishment of a community is essential. A highly predictable classroom is required if children are to learn to take responsibility and become a community of learners who help each other. Writing is an unpredictable act requiring predictable classrooms both in structure and response.

Children with learning disabilities often have histories of emotional problems. Many have become isolated and feel very little sense of community. They themselves may produce unpredictable classrooms. Their histories in taking responsibility are equally strewn with failure. Notions of choice and responsibility are threatening and require careful work on a broad front. The following ingredients help to build a structured, predictable community of more independent writers.

1. Write daily, at the same time if possible, for a minimum of thirty minutes.

2. Work to establish each child's topical turf, an area of expertise for each writer.

3. Collect writing in folders so that writers can see the accumulation of what they know. Papers do not go home; rather, the collected work is present in class for student, teacher, parent, and administrator to examine. Some writing is published in hardcover or some other durable form.

4. Provide a predictable pattern of teacher participation by sharing your own writing, moving in the midst of students during writing time, and responding in predictable structure to your students' writing.

5. End each writing time with children responding to one another's writing in a predictable format: receiving, questioning.

6. Set up classroom routines in which you examine the entire day to see which responsibilities can be delegated to the children. Solve room problems in discussion. The group learns to negotiate, whether in working with a draft or solving a classroom problem.

7. Continually point to the responsibilities assumed by the group, as well as the specifics of what they know.

The writing classroom is a structured, predictable room in which children learn to make decisions. The external structure is geared to produce a confident, internal thinking framework within which children learn what they know and develop their own initiative.

Continuing education of professionals

Most teachers have been drawn into process work because they have seen significant personal growth by their students with learning problems. Students who lacked confidence and initiative and were disenfranchised from literacy learn to write, share their writing with others, and take charge of their own learning. Although some teachers may wish to start work on the writing process based on this discussion, I suggest additional reading and work with their own writing.

The single most important help to teachers who work with young writers is work with the teacher's own writing. Both the National Writing Project and our work here at the University of New Hampshire stress work with the teacher's own writing. Thus teachers become acquainted with writing from the inside by actually doing it themselves. It would be unheard of for a piano teacher, a ceramicist, or an artist working with watercolors to teach someone their craft without practicing it themselves. Most of us have had little instruction in learning the craft of writing. We've written term papers, letters, and proposals, but we haven't worked with someone who has helped us to know what we know, then showed us how that knowledge is increased through the writing process.

I strongly encourage teachers to become involved in summer programs or consult their own universities to see if writing-process programs or courses are available. The following intensive summer programs concentrate on the teacher's own writing and the teaching of writing:

- Prof. Thomas Newkirk, English Department, Hamilton Smith Hall, University of New Hampshire, Durham, NH 03824

- Prof. Lucy Calkins, Teacher's College, Columbia University, New York, NY 10027

The National Writing Project has programs in almost all of the fifty states offering three- to four-week summer programs. Information about the National Writing Project is available from Dr. James Gray, National Writing Project, University of California at Berkeley, Berkeley, CA 94720.

Final reflection

Before children go to school, their urge to express is relentless. They learn to speak and to carry messages from one person to another. They burst into their homes to tell what just happened outside. They compose in blocks, play games, mark on sidewalks, and play with pencils or crayons. For most children, early audiences are receptive: adults struggle to make sense of the child's early attempts to communicate.

When children enter school, their urge to express is still present. A few enter already scarred from attempts to communicate with others. But the urge to be, to make a mark on the universe, has not left them. As children grow older and spend more time in school, many become still more disenchanted with writing. They can't keep up with the rest of the class and equate their struggles with handwriting, spelling, and early conventions as evidence that their ideas are unacceptable and that they are less intelligent than others. Even for these children, the urge to express, to make worthwhile contributions, to express a meaning that affects others does not go away.

The most critical factor for children with learning disabilities is the meaning-making question. Teachers need to first believe the children know important information, then work overtime to confirm for the child the importance of that information. The children see their teachers write; they see and hear them struggle for meaning on an easel or overhead projector as they compose before them. *The children become apprentices to the use of words.*

When children write, they make mistakes on the road to communicating their messages. The teacher's first response is to the meaning. Before a piece is completed, the teacher chooses one skill that will enhance the meaning of the piece still further. From the beginning, the teacher works to build a strong history for writers through collections of all their work, some publishing, and the writers' effective sharing with other members of the class.

Most teaching of writing is pointed toward the eradication of error, the mastery of minute, meaningless components that make little sense to the child. Small wonder. Most language arts texts, workbooks, computer software, and reams of behavioral objectives are directed toward the "easy" control of components that will show more specific growth. Although some growth may be evident on components, rarely does it result in the child's use of writing as a tool for learning and enjoyment. Make no mistake, component skills are important; if children do not learn to spell or use a pencil to get words on paper, they won't use writing for learning any more than the other children drilled on component skills. The writing-process approach simply stresses meaning first, and then skills in the context of meaning. Learning how to respond to meaning and to understand what teachers need to see in texts takes much preparation.

The writing process places high demands on the teacher. The room is carefully designed for developing student independence: Decisions are discussed, responsibilities assigned and assumed. Routines are carefully established with writing becoming a very important part of the room's routines. Initially, response to the child's writing is predictable, with receiving of the child's text followed by questions of clarification, the child's next step in the writing process.

Teachers who use the writing process to greatest advantage spend time working with their own writing. They read and become involved in many of the national institutes that are helping teachers use writing as a tool for their own learning. Soon they find their students' learning careers change as well.

References

Calkins, L.M. 1983. *Lessons from a Child*. Portsmouth, NH: Heinemann.

Graves, D. 1983. *Writing: Teachers and Children at Work*. Portsmouth, NH: Heinemann.

Hansen, J., T. Newkirk, and D. Graves, eds. 1985. *Breaking Ground: Teachers Relate Reading and Writing in the Elementary Classroom*. Portsmouth, NH: Heinemann.

Harste, J., C. Burke, and V. Woodward. 1984. *Language Stories and Literacy Lessons*. Portsmouth, NH: Heinemann.

Murray, D.M. 1983. *Write to Learn*. New York: Holt, Rinehart and Winston.

Newkirk, T., and N. Atwell, eds. 1982. *Understanding Writing*. Chelmsford, MA: The Northeast Regional Exchange.

Zinsser, W. 1980. *On Writing Well*. New York: Harper and Row.

13. Revaluing Readers and Reading

Kenneth S. Goodman

The term *readers in trouble* will be used here by the author to refer to all those who are not doing as well as they think (or someone else thinks) they should do in the development of reading proficiency. The common denominator among such readers is that they have become their own worst enemies. They have acquired a view that the world is populated by two kinds of people: those who can read and those who cannot, those who can learn and those who cannot. They believe that if they could just learn the phonics rules, just get enough word attacks, just master the skills, then they could do what good readers do easily and well. However, they know they cannot because something is wrong with them; they just do not learn like "normal" people.

The key to helping readers in trouble is to help them revalue themselves as language users and learners, and revalue the reading process as an interactive, constructive language process. They must set aside the pathological view of themselves, cast off the labels, and operate to construct meaning through written language using the strengths they have built and used in making sense of oral language or sign. To do that, they need support and help.

Reading: a unitary psycholinguistic process

Unfortunately, many educators have come to view reading as performance on tests, exercises, and workbooks. Teachers must put aside the instructional technology they have equated with reading and see reading instead as a process of making sense of written language, a receptive language process parallel to listening. In reading there is interaction between a reader and a written text and through it with a writer. What the reader brings to the text—experience, attitudes, concepts, cognitive schemes—is as important as what the author brought to it in creating it. The reader's act is creative too; meaning is created in response to the text.

Reading is a psycholinguistic process in which thought and language interact as the reader builds meaning. Readers are not the prisoners of their eyes.

They have brains with which they seek sense as they read—they predict and infer where the meaning is going, what sentence patterns are coming, what words and phrases are expected, and what the text will look like.

Within the continuous preoccupation with meaning, the reader selects from the available cues only those that are most useful, predicts on the basis of knowledge of language and the world, monitors his or her own success, and corrects when necessary to make sense. The reader is always tentative but confident. He or she is self-monitoring to make sure predictions are confirmed, but he or she is willing to take the risks necessary to move to meaning. Risk-taking, self-monitoring, and self-confidence are the essence of a revaluing program.

How is reading learned?

Learning language is largely a matter of finding its underlying system, inferring its rules, and then being able to use them to express meaning and to understand it. Language is easiest to learn when it is whole, relevant, real, in context, and functional for the user. In this respect, written language is no different from oral language.

One need not be unusually clever to learn to read and write any more than to learn oral language. Only when learners are distracted from meaning by instruction or confronted by materials full of abstract nonsense is a disadvantage created for those who may have mental or physical impairments. Learning letters is more difficult than learning words, which is more difficult than learning to remember or comprehend sentences. Understanding sets of unrelated sentences is more difficult than comprehending coherent stories or other meaningful texts.

Recent studies have demonstrated that children make a strong beginning as readers and writers as they encounter print in their environment and learn to understand its functions (Goodman 1980). As they see print used, they come to know what it is for and what it means. The key to learning is the universal search for order and comprehensibility that is characteristic of all humans. If educators can grasp that, then they can understand the tremendous strength that all pupils bring to learning to read and write. That understanding can help teachers to revalue nonachieving pupils and to understand that their failure is educators' failure to help them use the strengths they have. All children seem to be remarkable language learners outside of school. If they appear less successful in school, it is because learning language has been made too hard for them in the quest to make it easier.

Overemphasis on skills and teachers.   Skills have been the focus of the instructional programs troubled readers have repeatedly experienced. At the same time these pupils are trying to make sense of print they are also trying to read by the numbers: sounding out, attacking words, using skills. Getting the words right becomes more important, for them, than making sense. Every unfamiliar word becomes a major obstacle to be identified before going on.

The reader suffers from the "next-word syndrome"; each unconquered word is a symbol of defeat.

Readers in trouble are more likely to be the victims of too much skill use than not enough. They persevere on a single word, producing many nonword attempts before giving up. Many of them have had intensive instruction in phonics and word attacks over and over as they moved through remediation programs. Although the effect of this training shows in their phonic near misses, their miscues are often interpreted by diagnosticians as proof that more phonics is needed.

Readers in trouble also tend to look to the teacher to tell them what to do next. The pattern is to wait for a few seconds each time a problem word or phrase is encountered; then the teacher will supply the next word or an admonition to sound out the next word. The teacher may think he or she has helped by supplying the next word, but such repeated experiences only sustain the next-word syndrome and the basic feeling of defeat and inadequacy of the reader in trouble.

Scenario for failure.   Readers in trouble in literate societies with schools universally available have experienced repeated cycles of failure. The natural history of each cycle is something like this: The students are not doing well in school. The less well they do, the more intensively the teacher applies the program. If pupils are not doing well on worksheets, flash cards, skill drills, and remedial exercises, then the teacher repeats the same ones or provides supplementary, similar ones. If the usual amount of time spent on such activities is not paying off, then more time is provided for them, either at the expense of other, more meaningful aspects of the reading period, such as free reading time, or of other aspects of the curriculum, such as social studies, science, music, or art. If there is an aide available, then the aide is assigned to review and repeat with the readers in trouble what has not worked when the teacher did it. Recesses, lunch periods, after school time, even vacation periods are invaded in the name of helping readers in trouble to overcome their deficits.

Soon the classroom teacher gives up, and the child is referred for remediation. Remediation usually begins with a heavy battery of tests that confirm that the pupil is inadequately responding to skill instruction. The tests reveal patterns of weakness and deficiency. Remedial exercises are prescribed to eliminate the weaknesses. The exercises will tend to be more abstract and fragmented versions of what did not work in the classroom.

Sometimes at the beginning of remediation there appears to be an upsurge of achievement and a flicker of hope and enthusiasm on the part of the learner. The pupil enjoys the special attention, particularly if the remedial teacher is warm and encouraging. Somewhat improved scores are achieved. As the remediation continues, however, the learner sinks once more into despair. The abstractness of the fragmented skill drills leads to frustration. What was fresh and new is recognized as the same dull, repetitious, and tedious exercises that have not worked before. Pep talks and admonishments to try harder build personal guilt. Furthermore, the teacher shows resentment at the ingratitude of the learner for all the personal care and attention.

Meanwhile, back in the class, the remedial pupil is missing important learning opportunities; the time spent on remediation is the time classmates are spending building concepts, reading, writing, doing. So the learner in trouble, in the name of building basic skill competence, is deprived of rich school experience. Ironically, the pupil who rebels and acts out may be showing a healthier reaction than the pupil who withdraws or submits meekly to all this. At least such a rebel is showing a resistance to accepting full responsibility for failure.

Need for revaluing.   The answer to this dismal scenario is *revaluing*. The pupils must be helped to revalue themselves as learners. They must revalue the process of reading as the construction of meaning in response to print. They must come to be able to appreciate their own strengths, to recognize the productive strategies they already can use, and to build positively on those. They must come to put in perspective the interaction of themselves with an author through a text. Then they can put proper value on themselves, understand that no one can easily read and comprehend everything, and that what one knows before reading constrains what one can know after reading. They need to know that some texts are difficult to read because they are poorly written, and others because they contain new, complex ideas. They need to know that while everybody can find interesting, entertaining, or useful things in print, not everybody has to like everything they read. Finally, they need to realize that the easiest things for them to read are going to be the very ones they have the most interest in, the most background for, and that they get the most pleasure from.

Methods and materials for revaluing

Revaluing is not going to happen simply, easily, or quickly. It requires great patience and gentle support from teachers to help pupils in a long, slow rebuilding of the sense of self and sense of reading. Essentially, a revaluing program involves getting readers to read real, meaningful texts, to strengthen and gain new appreciation of the productive strategies that lead to comprehension, and to drop the nonproductive strategies.

Teachers can turn the conflict that readers in trouble experience every time they attempt to read into a positive force to achieve the revalued reading. Piaget (1971) talks about disequilibrium, a point in learning where the learner has unresolved conflicts and has not yet accommodated. Readers in trouble have been in this unbalanced state for so long that it has *become* reading for them.

From skills to meaning.   The very conditions of their discomfort, however, contain the seeds of productive resolution: Here is a written text created by an author to coherently represent a message; here is a reader trying to make sense of the text no matter what else he or she is doing. Patiently, in the context of supporting the reader's search for meaning, the teacher helps the reader to shift away from word identification, from sounding out, from teacher dependence. Patiently, the teacher helps the troubled reader to trust his or her own linguistic judgment, to have faith in the predictions and inferences that are coming to mind, to take risks, to self-monitor by constantly applying the key test: Does that make sense? Gradually the reader finds that the text is making sense. An accommodation takes shape in which graphophonic, syntactic, and semantic cues are used selectively to the extent that they are useful. Any exaggerated value attached to any one cue, cue system, or strategy gives way to putting each in its proper perspective.

Teacher as catalyst.   The teacher, carefully monitoring this conflict between productive and nonproductive strategies, between getting the next word and making sense, can be a catalyst. The teacher tips the balance by supporting the troubled readers' intuitions, by appreciating when something has worked or by asking a timely question at a point where the reader falters: *What's happening in the story? What do you already know about ———? Did that make sense? Why not?*

The teacher starts by learning about the learner. That does not mean diagnostic tests. It means asking learners what they read. It means inviting them to read a variety of things that vary in content, function, and complexity. It may mean, if the student has made some kind of start at becoming a reader, using some variation of miscue analysis (Goodman and Burke 1980). The teacher moves slowly and supportively to overcome the fear and despair. Often, as pupils relax, they reveal themselves to be much more capable than either they or the teacher had supposed.

One problem that may be faced at the beginning of a revaluing program is that the learners have so strongly internalized an expectation of how reading will be taught that they reject anything else. The pupil must come to trust the teacher and learn new ways of evaluating his or her own progress. The teacher must let the learner see how progress comes through a focus on trying to make sense of meaningful texts. This focus, of course, is near the center of revaluing.

Building self-confidence.   In starting to work with any reader in trouble, the teacher must take care not to assume that the pupil is devoid of reading ability. Thus, group or individual tests are untrustworthy: all they may reveal is the pupils' great fear of failure and the ease with which they become discouraged and give up. It is only after the pupil has relaxed and begun to fully participate that any trustworthy insights may be drawn. At the beginning, the instructional situation must be made completely nonthreatening. For some readers who are in serious trouble, it will be sufficient, as a beginning, to encourage them to follow as the teacher or aide reads.

As the reader gains confidence and begins to reveal interests, focus may shift to a variety of kinds of reading: signs, catalogues, manuals, menus, *TV Guide,* and the like. The teacher will seek evidence of particular pupil interest and supply materials, either narrative or expository, that will be highly motivating—materials that are interesting and will help build the reader's self-confidence.

To be successful in helping troubled readers, teachers must take their lead from the pupils. The teacher monitors the learner, letting the learner set the pace and direction, but offering the right help at the right time. This process is not unlike what parents do intuitively as they support the oral language development of preschool children.

Difficult textbooks.   Coping with school texts, especially in upper elementary and secondary grades, is a problem that most troubled readers face even as they are improving in their ability and self-confidence. In fact, it is often discouraging for pupils to realize that although they know they are reading much better, they still cannot handle grade-level texts. In dealing with this problem, as in all aspects of working with troubled readers, it is necessary for the teacher to be absolutely honest with the students. However, the pupils need to understand that it is not simply because they are ineffective readers that this problem occurs. Texts are difficult to read for many reasons. For example:

1. The texts may be poorly written. Too many subject matter texts are still written by authors who do not write clearly and concisely with the nature of the intended readers in mind. Often vocabulary is used that is unnecessarily technical and obscure or not properly developed, illustrated, and defined.

2. The texts may present too much information too superficially and too rapidly. This is, of course, a problem that will vary with the background and interest of the learner, and the skill of the teacher in providing experiences to help the pupils read and understand the text. The problem may not be a general weakness in reading but rather too little background for the concepts presented.

Helping pupils realize that it is not always their fault that they have trouble learning from textbooks is itself an important part of revaluing. Readers in trouble often think that good readers understand everything they read the first time they read it. Even when readers in trouble have reasonably good comprehension, they think they have failed because they cannot remember every little detail.

Strategies.   Readers in trouble also need other kinds of coping strategies:

1. Knowing how to read for the gist of a text rather than every detail, and knowing how to skim and survey materials to decide whether they are worth pursuing.

2. Knowing how to reread to focus on what is important in difficult materials.

3. Knowing how to frame questions to ask the teacher when they do not understand.

4. Knowing how to find information in simpler, easier to read reference books.

5. Knowing how to get information from sources other than books.

Part of the solution for dealing with difficult school texts lies with teachers understanding why pupils have difficulty with them. Misuse of texts by teachers (expecting pupils to learn from them without the teacher's help) is at least as important a cause of difficulty as ineffective reading.

Writing. Teachers of readers in trouble often find that as their pupils improve in reading, they become enthusiastic writers. Troubled readers are seldom expected to write much, so they usually have had little experience in writing. Their first efforts will look like those of near beginners, full of invented spelling and shaky mechanics and punctuation. Encouraging pupils to keep journals will create a nonpressured opportunity to write without worrying about accuracy. Pupils can then move on to a variety of other expository and creative writing. The key to writing development for troubled readers is to create a sense of *function* by focusing on the most useful and meaningful forms of writing.

Challenge for educators

It will not be enough to turn troubled readers into reluctant readers. Schools have produced too many people already who can read but do not choose to. Reading for troubled readers has been difficult, tedious, and nonproductive, and its acquisition has been associated with much embarrassment and pain. Teachers must patiently help such students to find reading materials that give them personal satisfaction and pleasure. They must help them realize that reading is something they can do when traveling, when waiting, when there is some time available for a quiet, personal activity, when there is nothing interesting on television or nobody to talk to. Pupils must reach the point where they choose to read when there is nobody to make them do it before educators can really claim success.

Teachers can make the difference in whether readers in trouble find their way out or not. However, to be successful they will need the help of parents, colleagues less directly concerned with literacy, and the pupils themselves. All must come to revalue the readers and the reading process.

References

Goodman, Y. 1980. "Roots of Literacy." In *Claremont Reading Conference Forty-fourth Yearbook,* edited by M. Douglas. Claremont, CA: Claremont Reading Conference.

Goodman, Y., and C. Burke. 1980. *Reading Strategies: Focus on Comprehension.* New York: Holt, Rinehart and Winston.

Piaget, J. 1971. *Psychology and Epistemology.* Translated by A. Rosin. New York: Grossman.

14. Notes from the Kitchen Table: Disabilities and Disconnections

Bonnie S. Sunstein

I am the mother of two "neurologically disabled" adolescents. During their lives, they have endured labels including "minimal brain dysfunction," "sensory motor dysfunction," "developmentally delayed," and "educable mentally retarded." But our kitchen looks pretty normal, and so do my kids. Most late afternoons, two bookbags lie yawning on the table, mounds of bent and wrinkled papers soak in wet rings from two after-school drinks. Two chewed pencils lie somewhere in each mess. And two teenagers lie around in the living room, snapping puns and insults back and forth to each other, reading the movie section and the weather report in the paper, and giggling at a jokebook. Which room holds their literacy? Where are their disabilities? On the bent papers in the kitchen? Or are they sprawled on the living room floor? Has anyone checked them for their abilities?

I've been a teacher of reading and writing longer than I've been a parent, and a reader and writer for longer than that. I am a student, a professor, a researcher. In each of these roles I agonize about our use of the word "disability." And I think about how we measure literacy disabilities and ignore literacy abilities. I live with two sides of this issue every day. At the university I work with people, books, and ideas about writing—some of the most respected, detailed, successful research in the English-speaking world. At the kitchen table I work with my children. And there are enormous gaps between what I see in my children's "special education" instruction and what I know about the processes of coming to write. I will examine those gaps here—how all this research could translate into classroom practice, and what happens when the bookbag comes home.

From what I see, school programs driven by tests to determine IEPs (Individualized Educational Plans), legally available to any student labeled with a disability, individualize for isolation. The plans categorize and classify students' deficits; they assess, describe, and measure what our students cannot do. The more disabled the student, the longer her IEP and the further away she moves from her chance at being part of a literate community. Isolated students have fewer opportunities for fluency, less trust in the value of their own ideas, and more outside control by their teachers and all the specialists demanded by the IEP. Inadvertently, a system meant to be inclusive—to protect our neediest students—is excluding them. The specialists and teachers know this best. In many schools, when "disabled" students move away from their desks, it is not to gather with others to share what they're learning. It is to leave the room to go for special help: resource rooms, remedial reading, physical therapy, occupational therapy, special tutorials, speech therapy. This is not only the story of severely handicapped students in special schools. In many public schools, this is the case as well.

The wheelchair incident: fact and fantasy

Steve, my son, attends a school for handicapped students (Sunstein 1990). One Monday morning, when the floors had been freshly buffed, another student, Jenny, rolled into class with a new electric wheelchair. Her hand, not always able to do what she wills it, got stuck on the forward control, and she careened all over the classroom. Mrs. Green froze; it was like watching a remote control bumping car, a bizarre Keystone Kops routine. Jenny bumped against one wall, spun around, bashed against the lockers, blasted some projects on the shelves. No one could stop her. She laughed; she was having a great time. Mrs. Green gave me a careful account of what happened next; she was both horrified and delighted.

Steve grabbed one of his extra thick pencils, held the eraser to his lower lip, and began a running sports commentary. "And now she's blasting the lockers, fans, watch out—this girl has power. She's shooting toward Mrs. Green. Will she flatten the teacher? Will she destroy the projects? Let's watch." Mrs. Green was able to guide Jenny out of danger—she could move obstructions in the room—but the situation belonged to the students. Jenny and Steve had control of the incident. It continued until Jenny's hand unlocked. Then the students sat down silently at their desks and attended to their workbooks.

That afternoon, the blue bookbag thunked on my kitchen table and spewed its daily contents. One worksheet had these words to unscramble:

cetupri (picture)

richa (chair)

kesd (desk)

Another one had four sequences of events out of sequence, and Steve's job was to fill in the blanks with "first," "next," and "last." The directions even took away his choice of words to describe the sequence; it told him what words to use:

_____ Then it took a nap.

_____ The kitten was hungry.

_____ It drank its milk.

Another page, called "Following Directions" in a section called "Understanding Structure and Purpose," offered a picture with two lines for writing below it. There were eight lines of directions:

Read and follow the directions to make a picture on the computer. Then write about what you have made. Draw a big box in the middle of the screen. Draw a triangle to fit exactly on top of the box. Stand a tall rectangle on the bottom line of the box. Put two small squares in the box. Put two trees next to the box. Then draw a path. Make it go up to the box. Put some flowers around the trees and the path.

Under the lines, there were two choices: "I made an animal," and "I made a house." Steve glared at the picture, insulted. His fat pencil hit the page harder than usual, and his hand was sure and determined. He scowled. "This is not a computer. This is a monitor," he wrote. It took thirty minutes to write those nine words, much longer than it did to follow the directions. He found the word "monitor" in a computer manual, and copied it. I was proud of him. He completed the worksheet wrong; he did not write "I made a house." The teacher wrote "excellent."

For Steve, whose neurons already scramble his brain, and who tries to feel thirteen whenever he can, literacy self-esteem comes when he circumnavigates his schoolwork. When the worksheets spill from his bookbag onto the kitchen table, he chews his pencil, bites the back of his hand, uses the worksheet to absorb the moisture from his drink glass, and goes into the living room to trade puns and swap insults with his sister. I watch to be sure he completes the school's requirements; their caring and attention has given him courage and self-esteem in other, personal ways. But I fantasize about what might have been.

That Monday morning, Steve's fluency had been quite real and sophisticated. His account of the wheelchair incident was packed with his own word choices and careful sequencing. It just never got down on paper; it wasn't on an IEP-driven worksheet. He chose great verbs: "blasting," "shooting," "flatten." He used action: "watch out," "blasting the lockers, fans." He made predictions and developed suspense: "Will she flatten the teacher? Will she destroy the projects? Let's watch." He made an informed judgment: "This girl has power." His play-by-play commentary was sequenced without the sequencing words "first," "next," and "last." A curriculum based on writing would value this incident. His teacher valued this incident for him. But no traditional IEP would expect such sophistication from a student like Steve. According to the tests, his measured "skill levels" are not sufficient for such "higher-order tasks" in the cognitive domain.

Jenny, too, achieved some self-esteem that morning, and a chance for literacy. She was proud of her triumph as an independent person. She had something to say about it, too. She had held her classmates and her teacher in suspension for a time, learning their concern for her—learning the power her new electronic freedom allowed her in her own community. As she got back to work on the worksheets designated for her that day, her classmates whispered a lot of questions. What did it feel like? Did she know how to stop herself? Was it like running? Could she reach the projects on the shelves? Would she have hit Mrs. Green? She was special. They were curious. But she was shushed into quiet, and she bent over her desk, her fist holding her thickened pencil, quietly straining marks to fill in the blanks someone else had chosen for her.

So how do I fantasize this scenario as a celebration of the literacy of two young teenagers? In a classroom that builds writing and reading from students' own ideas, like many I see, this would have been an opportunity for writing, for teaching inside the classroom community. Mrs. Green might have stopped and asked everyone to write for ten minutes about what had just happened. Jenny might have begun writing a piece on the power her new wheelchair gave her. She might have continued it with a detailed description of her new wheelchair's electronic potential, or a comparison/contrast with her old one. Or she might have written about power—or lack of power—for the physically disabled. Or maybe a poem about how speed feels. It would have been her choice; she would have sought the information, but with time enough, everyone would have learned from it. Steve would not have been able to put his words on a page with his own hand, but he could have reconstructed his sports commentary with someone's help, learned something new about sports writing by researching in sports books or reading articles. He could have looked at his verb choices, maybe, and dictated an account of another sports event to his tutor or a classmate who could type it or write it down, examining action verbs. Later, if either of them had chosen to redraft these pieces, they might have shared the final product with other students, reconstructing, expanding, redefining the incident. The teacher, or another student with a different specialty, might have nudged out a few more details after listening.

In any case, both students would have shared their reflections of what had happened with the group and turned it into an occasion for literacy. The whole classroom community could have learned a lot from Jenny's explorations into power and Steve's research about sportscasting. Writing processes are a series of operations—not always the same series—leading to the solution of a problem, the answer to a question—not the same problem, not the same question. They begin with people who notice things—not always people with the same kinds of abilities; not always the same things noticed. Good worksheets (frames, plans, outlines) come *after* the idea, and then each "worksheet" is a unique plan.

Steve's IEP is thirty-six pages long. The first psychologist, who understood his differences as a learner, wrote: "Steve's academic achievement is better measured by classroom progress than by formal, standardized, normed tests." After the team meeting to design the IEP, the psychologist's words were translated into: "In general, Steve does best when a single task is broken down as much as possible into separate steps, each of which is a single process. Trying to do two steps at once is usually a problem." The school's functional translation on the IEP looked like this: "He can best handle fill-in worksheets when presented with no more than two choices. On material relevant to him, comprehension is good, and he can do a good job of sequencing." Hence, the worksheets. He copies someone else's words; with his brain that's already scrambled, he unscrambles real words that have been scrambled deliberately; he identifies inaccurate pictures. And there is no time left for his ideas.

Three myths and one research paper

My daughter, Amy, is a little less disabled than Steve. Her IEP is only twenty-six pages long. Each page lists thirteen to fifteen objectives, and there are five pages devoted to reading and writing. It is characterized by such statements as:

The student will read orally (mastery is achieved at 85% accuracy) those words which contain a CVCE syllable in the final position and have 3–5 syllables from a list (example: infantile, magnitude, contaminate).

Under the category "Written Expression," two of the objectives state:

> Given a list of notes, the student will organize them by sequencing a category orally, or in writing without assistance, within ten minutes.

> Given a topic and list of notes, and topic sentence, the student will write a clincher sentence to conclude the paragraph, within three minutes.

These are admirable skills; I wish I could have used them so mechanically as I wrote this chapter, but fluency comes differently for different tasks, especially when we are working with new ideas. Amy reads *Rolling Stone* magazine, constructs long and carefully classified lists, writes elaborate letters. The social notes I find in her jeans pockets show a range of passion, exposition, narrative, and argumentation far stronger than the structured paragraphs she prewrites and edits for school. In school, though, there is no time for novels because as one teacher told me, "there are too many skills to remediate." It makes me consider three myths the IEPs suggest:

> MYTH I: In reading and writing, fluency must come before comprehension or meaning is possible.

> MYTH II: Independent reading is something to do at home; independent writing is done in school with teacher-set guidelines, structures, and assignments.

> MYTH III: Writing is governed by a progression and combination of skills that doesn't vary according to the genre or the message.

With these myths and IEPs as goals for reading and writing (Cioffi 1990), it's easy to see how students continue to fail and special ed teachers burn out. These goals are hard to accomplish; literacy isn't so linear.

With time, some help, and a word processor, here's what Amy did for social studies, a subject not bound by the IEP's goals for remediation. She wondered "What was life like for women during World War II?" Amy interviewed her grandmothers over the phone, looked at pictures, letters, and short written accounts from World War II in three reference books. She combined what she learned and wrote a four-page paper, with these subheadings: "Why Women Had to Work," "Jobs Women Had," and "Life for Women at Home." A few excerpts:

A poster from 1944 shows three women doing three different jobs. It says "Soldiers Without Jobs." . . . 780,000 women worked DURING WWII. They worked on farms, and they worked in shipyards and aircraft plants. My grandmother's friend Betty, an artist, helped design airplanes for Sun ship company. Her cousin Carol drove an ambulance. My other grandmother was a telephone operator, and once she cut off an important person from Washington. . . . It was awful to keep food in the house. They had rationing, which meant they could only get a few kinds of food each week. They ate grilled liverwurst and fake butter. They could only buy one pair of shoes every nine months. . . .

It took Amy more than ten minutes to sequence and organize her notes, more than three minutes to write a "clincher" conclusion. But the paper is literate, fluent, and answers a real question with information she gathered, and she knew she was writing for an audience. Her grandmothers and her social studies teacher were enthusiastic readers. Amy's fluency isn't complete, but she has meaning and comprehension. She can't wait for reading or spelling to get to writing—it's all connected. Students are shut off from fluency by disconnecting them from opportunities. Learning disabled students *stay* broken, like the sentences their worksheets ask them to construct.

What we already know

We want all students to be fluent with language, and for students with disabilities, fluency comes harder. For students with school-identified disabilities, language experience is too disconnected from daily life. These students need peers and adults in naturally literate settings, who will listen to their ideas, help them enjoy appropriate social behaviors that come naturally to others, painfully to them. They *do* have problems generating and absorbing language. They *do* need extra help. It takes sophisticated thinking to link a litany of C-V-C-E patterns (consonant-vowel-consonant-ending) to last week's canoe trip, a favorite novel or a burning interest in rock music, a journal of science observations, or a letter to someone. For these "at-risk" students, there are very few risks they can take. Their path toward independence is cluttered. With the best of intentions, school plans and specialists inadvertently control their connections and limit their choices. For them, each day looks like a fill-in-the-blanks worksheet.

Donald Graves (1985) reminds us that testing practices set standards too low in schools. And our standards for disabled students are set even lower. It is essential that we begin to pay attention to connecting their lives with their language. We need to begin by asking the question Graves likes to ask: What is writing for? And, most important for them, What can students with school disabilities already do? What literacy abilities do they already have?

In the last twenty years, our research has taught us that writing is not an isolated task—it is a social act: that in order to write, students need other people around them who are writing and reading, talking and listening—who want to learn things. Some research generalizes, to see similarities among human beings. Other research moves us toward seeing their differences. Our case study research, conducted over long periods of time in real classrooms, has shown us a lot about differences in writers, and it is a close look at the writers themselves—through their teachers and participant observers in their classrooms—that can give us the information we need to suggest ways to help.

Nancie Atwell (1988) has called these students the "ghosts in her school," the students who were never in her classes because they were in the resource room "being remediated." When she began to include them in the bustling, connected literacy of her classroom, they set their own standards higher— independently, and in their own time, with the help of their community. One of her students, Laura, had a big IEP, a small ego, and a heap of related social problems. In a short eighth-grade year, she grew far beyond the goals set by the school's IEP. Laura wrote letters to an author, wrote interviews and poems, not to mention all the reading, speaking, and listening she did with new respect from and interest in her classmates. Laura superseded the "written language skills" set out by her IEP and demonstrated complex competencies.

Our studies see what happens when students are included instead of isolated, encouraged as whole people instead of analyzed as broken language machines. William Wansart's case study of Jessica (see Chapter 10) is a dramatic illustration of a disabled student who, when allowed daily, predictable time and help with writing and reading in a normal classroom, eventually became a writer and a resource for her fellow students—a specialist in fiction and pets. It took Jessica until April to share her writing, but she did it, and the following year she met success in September.

Cindy Matthews' (1990) study of Joey, a young nonreader from a home of adult oral storytellers, shows that his writing, over time, led him to be able to read. Joey's writing reflected oral story elements of repetition, parallelism, sound play, and word play. Joey's storytelling, with its traditional conventions of narrative, shared in a writing workshop, brought him to fluency and to reading.

Many of these students come to school without much that's whole for them: not sports teams, not dances or friends. Their parents worry more than they brag, and then there is the testing—doctors, psychologists, and school systems. We know that even very young children can construct elaborate arguments and articulate in sophisticated rhetorical forms (Newkirk 1989). Our case studies show that, given the opportunity, so can older students with disabilities. They need to be *inside* their ideas, writing about them and doing it often. I suggest that all remediation plans ought to include a careful look at what level of natural fluency the students are allowed. They need to see the patterns in what they know. It's in the planning and coaching, in the extending of a piece of writing that we—and they—can see growth. Students need to be involved in evaluating their own literate productions, reflecting on what they know, what they've learned, and how they've learned it. There is no greater personal strength.

Philip M. Ferguson and Adrienne Asch (1989) note that there is still a scholarly neglect of the direct, personal accounts of disabled individuals and their parents as a legitimate source of information for policy analysis and service reform, and it is their contention that personal narratives constitute a large and neglected source of data for understanding how schools could better support disabled children and their families. Ferguson and Asch are both researchers and teachers; one is a parent of a disabled child and the other is a disabled person herself. They offer an eloquent reminder that we need to close those gaps between the abilities of the teenagers sprawled on the living room floor and the disabilities that glare from the IEPs:

The most important thing that happens when a child is born with disabilities is that a child is born. The most important thing that happens when a couple becomes parents of a child with disabilities is that a couple becomes parents. These two statements seem almost tautologous. Yet, the history of professional approaches to the personal experience of disability by parents and children creates an unfortunate but enduring need to reaffirm their truth. Whether in medicine, education, psychology, or social work, the professional approach to people living with a disability has repeatedly seemed to want to reverse biology. Parents and children become the adjectives, disability the noun. (1989, 108)

References

Atwell, Nancie. 1988. "A Special Writer at Work." In *Understanding Writing: Ways of Observing, Learning, and Teaching K-8,* 2nd edition, edited by Thomas Newkirk and Nancie Atwell. Portsmouth, NH: Heinemann.

Cioffi, Grant. 1990. Personal communication. Education Department, University of New Hampshire.

Graves, Donald H. 1984. *A Researcher Learns to Write.* Portsmouth, NH: Heinemann.

———. 1985. "All Children Can Write." *LD Focus* 1 (1): 36–43.

Ferguson, Philip M., and Adrienne Asch. 1989. "Lessons from Life: Personal and Parental Perspectives on School, Childhood, and Disability." In *Schooling and Disability, Eighty-Eighth Yearbook of the National Society for the Study of Education,* Part II, edited by D. Bicklen, D. Feguson, and A. Ford. Chicago: University of Chicago Press.

Matthews, Cindy. 1990. "Joey's Storying: A Linguistic Analysis of an Oral and a Written Story of a Nonmainstream Second Grader." Unpublished paper. Writing Lab, University of New Hampshire.

Newkirk, Thomas. 1989. *More than Stories: The Range of Children's Writing.* Portsmouth, NH: Heinemann.

Sunstein, Bonnie S. 1990. "On Home Town Alienation." *Reading Instruction Journal* 33 (2): 35–39.

15. Many Ways of Knowing

Linda Hoyt

Michael, a first-grade Chapter 1 student, announced on his first day of our class that he couldn't read and that we—my instructional assistant and I—couldn't make him. At first, it seemed that his proclamation could be true. He resisted all of our efforts to entice him into the world of print. As his Chapter 1 teacher, I was puzzled by his attitude; the other first graders seemed to find so much pleasure in the literacy experiences they encountered in our resource room. Michael's mother reported that he enjoyed listening to stories at home but that he seemed fearful of attempting to read or write on his own.

On a day when each Chapter 1 student was invited to bring a toy to school and write about it, Michael brought a G.I. Joe man. He gleefully talked about his G.I. Joe man and drew pictures of it, but steadfastly refused to write about it. While all of his Chapter 1 classmates were writing, Michael continued to draw and gaze at a typewriter where a parent volunteer was typing our newest student-authored books. Capitalizing on his interest, I decided to invite him to type about the picture he had drawn. Michael typed, "My G.I. Joe man is hitting another man. Next time you better not mess with me" (see Figure 15–1). With a grin as broad as his face, Michael rushed to share his story with the rest of his group. His first attempt at writing felt wonderful, and he decided to immediately publish it into a book. Michael carried his book everywhere, reading it to anyone who would listen.

Because he was motivated, felt safe, and had an opportunity to reshape his prior knowledge through written language, Michael became a new member of the literacy club (Smith 1986). Two weeks later Michael appeared with a letter for me (see Figure 15–2). The magic of reading and writing was inside of him all along; he just needed confidence to begin applying his fledgling understandings about print. Michael became a willing participant in the writing experiences of his home room as well as the resource room. He had learned the joy of taking a risk and succeeding. He had learned the joy of self-expression through written language.

Nine-year-old Mandy, a student with learning disabilities complicated by a language disorder, worked with a group in our resource room to read and act

Figure 15–1

Michael's typed caption to his drawing of G. I. Joe.

```
mi je ijoman ishitenanonothr man .
nixtimubenotmeswno   me
```

out elephant stories. We drew pictures of elephants, interviewed elephant keepers at the zoo, and wrote ABC books with facts about elephants. As a result, Mandy and her group could expound in great detail about the difference between African and Asian elephants, explain the social nature of an elephant herd, and dramatize the lumbering gait of a baby elephant. In spite of their reputation as low-functioning students, these children eagerly devoured fiction as well as nonfiction materials. They actively engaged in producing books filled with information about elephants, written descriptions of elephants, and readers theater scripts based on elephant stories. Through a variety of expressive arts, these young learners were able to process meaning in ways that allowed them to deepen and expand their understanding. The opportunity to translate their information about elephants into clay, paint, and oral language allowed them to utilize their strengths. During these sessions, Mandy's eyes sparkled. She eagerly read, wrote, and even brought additional resources from home to support our research on elephants. This child who seldom spoke outside of the resource room used her language to learn, to clarify, and to share.

My visits to the classroom showed a very different side of Mandy. She listlessly sat and twirled her pencil or stared out the window while other students worked diligently in basal workbooks. She moved as slowly as she dared through the classroom assignments, leaving her teacher unsure of how much she was willing or able to do. The eager resource room child was cut adrift from the things she did well. Because workbooks and correct answers were the only acceptable form of communication in the classroom, Mandy was unable to create a link between her world and the learning for which she was reaching.

For Mandy and Michael, events in the classroom often did not have a clear connection to events that made sense within the culture of their childhood. They saw literacy learning as an obstacle to be conquered rather than a vehicle for accomplishing their personal goals in life. Both learners were in need of consistent literacy experiences that engaged them with a variety of communication systems so that they could make use of their communicative strengths while gaining control over written language.

Jerome Harste (1988) describes transmediation as a process of moving information from one communication system to another. This process causes the brain to activate both hemispheres as the information is analyzed, evaluated, and then reformed to be shared in a new way. Attempts to express messages through a variety of media encourage learners to generate new meanings and to expand existing ones. Michael experienced transmediation as he moved

Figure 15–2
Michael's letter to his teacher.

Dear Mrs Hoyt
I liked The pizza
And I like you
Thank yon for
helping me.

his knowing about G.I. Joe men from the oral mode to written language. Mandy transmediated her knowing about elephants into drama and oral discussion.

Meaningful writing, talking, drama, and art offer alternative modes for self-expression. When we encourage at-risk students to move information from one communication system to another, we offer them a way to make use of their strengths rather than always focusing on their weaknesses. We support their feelings of self-worth by making success more attainable. For example, to show what she knew about elephants through the media of clay, Mandy had to take a new psychological stance toward her information. She had to determine the finite details of her knowing and develop a new perspective toward the information as she took on the role of the artist. To shape her communication from a lump of gray clay, she was continually searching her own knowledge bank for the details that she needed to represent in her model.

To help at-risk children make a connection between school and the real world, we must make an unrestrained effort to link learning to real-life purposes. Knowing about reading and writing isn't enough. We must know how to use reading and writing. We must find ways to engage the learner's affective as well as cognitive self through a wide variety of interactions and experiences in many kinds of literacies. Comprehension cannot be fostered by transmitting information from the page to the children's heads or by drilling the children with questions. Learning happens when one creates a personal interpretation. This interpretation can take the form of a feeling, an artistic expression, or a rush of language as the individual connects to the new information. The important point is that the learner makes the information personal and internalizes a connection between what is new and what is already known (Bussis 1989). Unfortunately, children who have difficulty learning to read and write are often subjected to an endless regime of skill and drill, workbooks, and flashcards. Characteristically, these are children who need to utilize their tactile, auditory, visual, and kinesthetic senses. Yet they sit at a desk and attempt to cope with tasks that bear little resemblance to their world or their developmental needs.

The expressive arts offer learners many ways of knowing. Through transmediation of information, children can utilize their strengths in learning while bridging the gap to their deficits.

Speaking and listening

At one time, quiet classrooms were considered the ideal environment for learning. However, as we have learned more about the social nature of learning and consider the implications of transmediation, we must remember that talking is an expressive art. It is essential to provide opportunities for children to talk about what they are learning and the strategies they are using for inquiry. We must give them opportunities to engage in the kinds of discussion that adults might experience, but questions and dialogue need to be genuine acts of communication and not simply a rote reaction to situations controlled by the teacher. Through this type of interaction, we can help our children translate their knowing to the oral language system of our culture. We can help them to delve more deeply as thinkers.

Talking is a powerful tool for clarifying ideas and verifying information. Through conversation, we can often see issues more clearly, from a different viewpoint, or move to higher levels of creativity (Graves 1983). Children need to understand that talking is a tool for learning. Just as they talk together while building a creation from Legos or blocks, children need time to talk together while they are focused on acts of reading and writing. Together they can consider the potential meaning of a passage, clarify their written expression, and reflect on the processes that help them to interact with their world.

Similar to the responsive discussions that occur during writer's workshop, a group of students were discussing *Tuck Everlasting,* by Natalie Babbit. As they considered the theme of eternal life, a sixth grader by the name of Susan said that she would want to be twenty-one forever. She thought it would be the perfect age because she could drive a car, live independently, and be her own boss. Cheryl countered by suggesting that Susan think about what it would be like to have all of her friends changing and maturing, her potential children looking older than she would, and so on. Through conversation, these students were helping each other to grow and develop as reflective thinkers and communicators. Similarly, when Michael was drawing about his G.I. Joe man, he chatted continually with his partner, making comments such as: "I am drawing a field jacket on my man so he can carry his canteen and supplies." "Can you tell he is standing on a mountain?"

Children need plenty of opportunities to engage in meaningful communication with adults and peers. They need to revise and clarify messages, to engage in appropriate interactions, and to experience elaboration and expansion of their own language. Through these verbal experiences, oral language grows and clears the path for interaction with more complex written language structures.

Art

As in the example of Mandy and her clay elephant, visual arts such as drawing, painting, and collage can offer alternative ways for a child to express knowing and to explore his or her own inner language. Interactions with the visual arts are also laden with motivators for children. Because the study of literacy is too often focused on words, it is important to look back to the images and feelings that precede the words, to explore the relationships between the way children see the world and the way it is interpreted in print (Elkind 1988).

To draw a picture about a story, learners must draw upon both the affective and the cognitive domains. They must think about all of the events in a story before selecting one that merits further attention. The event must then be analyzed for elements of setting, characterization, and details before a picture can be drawn. A seemingly simple task actually requires a great deal of evaluation, analysis, and attention to detail.

For children who have difficulty with written and oral language, artistic expression focused on a learning experience can help them to organize thinking and rehearse for more traditional means of expression. Michael's drawing of his G.I. Joe man helped him to focus on his topic, consider relevant details, and think about the written language that was to follow. Mandy's clay elephant had wrinkles in its trunk, nails on its toes, and small ears to indicate its Asian heritage. By the time Mandy finished her clay elephant, she had internalized the small bits of information and was able to write a long descriptive piece that demonstrated her confidence with the topic.

Sharing information through art can also be facilitated through development of student-made bulletin boards, murals, dioramas, mobiles, and paintings. As the artistic expression takes shape, the learner can internally process the information in his or her own way. While these activities should not significantly reduce the amount of time spent reading and writing, they can be a very powerful support system for a reading and writing program.

Drama

Drama is an essential element of a language and literacy program (Booth 1987). In drama, the children invent most of the dialogue and action, drawing ideas from the environment, their reading, and their background knowledge. They use their bodies and their voices as ways of communicating their understandings.

The kinesthetic involvement that is a natural part of drama offers a very powerful connection for special needs students. The bodily motion brings their attention into full focus and helps them interpret meaning in nonverbal ways. After reading *Theodor and Mr. Balbini,* by Petra Mathers, two Chapter 1 boys were demonstrating how Theodor and Mr. Balbini related to each other. The boy representing Mr. Balbini hung his head and slumped his shoulders to demonstrate Mr. Balbini's submissiveness. The boy who was Theodor stood on a chair, put his hands on hips, and glowered down at Mr. Balbini. The understanding of the relationship between the characters was clear. These students had gone far beyond sequence and events. Through drama, they shared sophisticated intuitions about characterization and inferential relationships. This performance provided an interesting contrast to the boys' poor showing on the rote-level questioning that characterized their workbooks and classroom reading groups.

After enacting a story, students can be encouraged to re-create the meaning with pictures or writing. These retellings often reflect powerful new understandings of the story and are punctuated with specific details of setting and mood. Furthermore, because of the dramatic interaction that preceded the writing, every child is able to write with clarity and purpose. The combination of drama, body movement, and discussion lays a strong foundation for writing and helps special learners verify their information through several communication systems before commiting it to writing.

Drama can be a powerful reading strategy for learners who need additional support with literacy development. Before reading a text, students listen to the teacher read as a demonstration of fluency and expression. They retell the story in their own words, discuss its interesting points, and then act it out. This process helps the learner internalize the language patterns of the author, clarify the meaning, and develop the expectation that the print must make sense. One of the largest differences between good and poor readers is that good readers expect the print to make sense. Poor readers are often happy just to say the words in order (Wong 1985). Drama as a reading strategy emphasizes the meaning of the passage and enables the reader to interact with the text with fluency and understanding.

Readers theater

Readers theater is a way to interpret a story using the text as it is written. Different from drama, in which body motion portrays a great deal of the meaning, readers theater is totally dependent on the ability of the reader's voice to capture the listener. The readers have the task of using reading rate, intonation, and emphasis on the meaning-bearing cadences of our language to make the print come alive. While there are many published scripts that turn favorite literature selections into readers theater, the most effective scripts often are designed by the students.

After reading a selection, groups of children can list the main characters and then select events from the story to be used in the readers theater presentation. As each portion of the text is selected, the students determine who is speaking and whether they will use all or part of that particular section. This analysis of the text stimulates reflection on the key points of the story and can generate insightful observations about the author's style.

Readers theater is often presented with only one student reading each character's part. This format creates an interesting presentation, but the result is that few children have the opportunity to engage in the reading. To provide a reading response for every child in class, divide the children into small groups. Each group is responsible for rehearsing and chorally reading the dialogue of a character or the lines spoken by the narrator. This format gives every child a role, encourages repeated readings for fluency, and allows the group to set a pace that helps even the most disabled readers to experience reading at a rate that approximates oral speech.

Students can also use the readers theater format without using a prepared script. An overhead transparency made from a page in a story (see Figure 15–3, for example) allows the entire group to read while the teacher directs their attention. The teacher may want to have the students chorally read the narration while the teacher demonstrates voices for the dialogue. The transparency can also be used to help the students practice determining who is speaking within each set of quotation marks. To accomplish this, circle key words within the text and have the students work in partners to decide who is speaking and what clues helped them to identify the speaker. The transparency allows the entire group to focus on one part of the script at a time and to discuss strategies for chorally reading the text. After rehearsing on the overhead, fluent and delayed readers alike will experience success when reading the dialogue from their own copies of the text.

Figure 15–3

Overhead transparency of a page from a story.

Reaching the edge of the mantle, they saw a solid, rocky landscape and began to feel some heat. As the nose drilled deeper, it made a grinding sound that vibrated throughout the ship. The heat began to increase and Brian cried out, "time for the air conditioning!"

In response, Dr. Blow said, "It is also time for the rudders that I attached to this vehicle to prepare for the (liquid) outer core."

"(Yes) Sir!"

Suddenly the ship plunged into the intense heat and flowing activity of the outer core. It gave a sensation of floating as the ship flowed with the molten rock.

"I've (never) been so hot!" cried Andy.

"It's the most awesome sight I've ever seen," breathed Brian.

Feeling that they would melt from the intensity of the heat, the crew turned on the air conditioning full blast and surged toward the inner core.

---

reprinted with permission from the author, Brenden Hoyt, age 11

Music and dance

As their teacher strummed softly on the strings of his guitar, the students in the elementary learning center sang, "Mr. Sun, Sun, Mr. Golden Sun. Won't you shine down on me." Their bodies moved with the beat of the music, and every child's attention was on the lyrics. Even those who had not mastered all of the words stayed with the beat of the song and heartily joined in on the chorus. These students had been identified as having a wide variety of handicapping conditions, including language disorder, mild retardation, and cerebral palsy, yet there was not a child in the group who did not feel successful during the song. Building on the children's strong sense of connection to the rhythm and music, the words of the song became a literacy experience. The children learned to read the lyrics in a big book they made themselves, and they illus-trated small book versions to take home. They learned about letter/sound relationships while manipulating the phrases and words of the song in a pocket chart. As their interactions with the song continued over time, they tried writing new verses of the song, devised motions to use while singing the words, and experimented with rhythm instruments.

Music and rhythm have a powerful lure for children that not only can motivate them but can also help them connect to literacy experiences. The predictable patterns of music help stir memory and allow children to remember chunks of text that they might not otherwise be able to recall, as evidenced by the large number of kindergarten teachers who teach children to sing their telephone number or address while trying to memorize it.

Electronic keyboards and rhythm instruments can be rhythmical fluency builders in developing readers. By choosing a preprogrammed rhythm that matches the appropriate rate for a story, students can chorally read to musical accompaniment. The result is dramatic reading with a strong sense of theme. To keep up with the rate of the music, students often read faster, naturally reading past unknown words to maintain the pace and the rhythm. Students also enjoy using rhythm instruments to punctuate special points in a story. They might select a certain instrument for each character in the story or use special chords to accentuate key events. Rhythm instruments can also be used to establish a background tempo for reading poems and stories.

Music and dance together with mime offer the additional benefit of involving kinesthetic action. Students can create hand motions and full-body movements to enhance their enjoyment of favorite songs or stories. As with drama, this full-body engagement increases the likelihood of complete engagement and lays the groundwork for in-depth literacy experiences. After dancing their way through a story or a song, students are more likely to remember the events. They are able to write about their experience of movement or about the story itself.

Peter and the Wolf is an example of a story told through music that is particularly inviting as a dance experience. Children love to close their eyes and try to visualize the hungry wolf chasing the fat duck while Peter frantically attempts to intervene. They love to move their bodies to reflect the changing tempo, swaying softly with the grass in the meadow or frantically climbing up the tree to escape the running wolf.

A growing number of books that have been created from popular songs are appearing on the shelves of bookstores and libraries. Emerging readers enjoy the instant success that they have when they pick up *There Were Ten in the Bed* or *Old MacDonald Had a Farm*.

Conclusion

More than once, classroom teachers have asked me why I use valuable resource room time to work with clay and write books. They believed that resource room students needed to spend large amounts of time working on skill books if they were to become stronger readers. I found that these students were already skilled at circling, underlining, and filling in the blanks. Yet they were struggling as readers.

In the resource room we focused on creating connections through the expressive arts and made sure that literacy experiences were as authentic and as meaningful as we could make them. Using their own natural abilities as communicators, our students began to believe in themselves as readers and writers, and even began to perform well on standardized measures of achievement. The classroom teachers, parents, and I came to understand that learning isn't segmented into isolated subject areas in the minds of children. The world is a connected, integrated whole, and their learning must be seen in the same way.

Through a variety of expressive arts, our young learners were able to process meaning in ways that allowed them to deepen and expand their understanding. Most remarkably, because they first had the opportunity to translate their information into drama, clay, paint, and oral language, they were able to write with a strength and conviction normally expected of the highest functioning students.

Classrooms that offer children a variety of communication systems facilitate learning in ways that stimulate the imagination, enhance language learning, and deepen understanding. These communication options present learners with the opportunity to create a tighter link between themselves and new learning. When children are actively engaged with the expressive arts, their attention spans often seem to lengthen; smiles replace groans and looks of frustration. When literacy learning is linked to activities that flow from the culture of childhood, learners read and write with more conviction and power.

References

Anderson, R. C., el al. 1985. *Becoming a Nation of Readers: The Report of the Commission on Reading*. Urbana, IL: Center for the Study of Reading.

Babbitt, Natalie. 1985. *Tuck Everlasting*. New York: Farrar, Straus and Giroux.

Booth, David. 1987. *Drama Words*. Toronto: Language Study Centre.

Bussis, Anne M. 1989. "Burn It at the Casket: Research, Reading Instruction, and Children's Learning of the First R." In *Whole Language: Beliefs and Practices, K-8*. Washington, DC: National Education Association.

Christie, James. 1990. "Dramatic Play: A Context for Meaningful Engagements." *Reading Teacher* 43(8): 542–545.

Edelsky, Carole. 1982. "Living in the Author's World: Analyzing the Author's Craft." *The California Reader* 21:14–17.

Elkind, David. 1988. *The Hurried Child*. Reading, MA: Addison-Wesley.

Graves, Donald H. 1983. *Writing: Teachers and Children At Work*. Portsmouth, NH: Heinemann.

Hansen, Jane. 1987. *When Writers Read*. Portsmouth, NH: Heinemann.

Harste, Jerome, et al. 1988. *Creating Classrooms for Authors*. Portsmouth, NH: Heinemann.

Lioni, Leo. 1984. "Before Images." *The Horn Book,* November/December 1984: 726–734.

Paterson, Katherine. 1981. *Gates of Excellence*. New York: E. P. Dutton.

Rhodes, Lynn, and Nancy Shanklin. 1989. "Comprehension Instruction as Sharing and Extending." *Reading Teacher* 42 (6):496–500.

Routman, Regie. 1988. *Transitions.* Portsmouth, NH: Heinemann.

Seigel, Marjorie. 1984. "Sketch to Stretch." *Reading, Writing and Caring.* New York: Richard C. Owen.

Smith, Frank. 1978. *Reading Without Nonsense.* New York: Teachers College Press.

Wilson, Marilyn. 1988. "Critical Thinking: Repackaging or Revolution?" *Language Arts* 65:543–551.

Wong, Bernice. 1985. Oral presentation given in Beaverton, Oregon.

16. Only Skeletons Belong in Closets

Janis Ivanowsky Bailey

"I thought you were a reading specialist. Why are you teaching third grade?"

"Only skeletons belong in closets," I reply. "Removing students from the classroom just doesn't make sense. As I thought about working in a separate room to do individual and small-group teaching, I realized the pull-out model only served to point out students' weaknesses. Since my intentions are to build self-esteem and reading strengths, I decided to move back to the classroom."

I have answered that question many times, and each time I reflect on my evolution as a teacher. I began as a zealous first-year classroom teacher. After five years, I moved to a new job as a reading specialist, working in a small room fixing children. Now I am a third-grade classroom teacher, building a classroom community where everyone is a learner and a resource for the others.

Here is the story of my evolution.

Twenty-seven second graders filled my first classroom seventeen years ago. I was ready to use all I had learned about individualized reading and creative writing to help my students love reading and learning. Then I was distracted.

On my desk were neat piles of readers, 2-1's and 2-2's, with descendents of my childhood friends, Dick, Jane, and Sally. Nostalgia set in, and I remembered my feelings of pride when I learned to read from those books. I dove into the pile of books and felt right at home with those old familiar texts. As I rummaged through the rest of the materials on the desk, I discovered a spiral-bound teacher's book that accompanied the students' texts. Imagine! This must have been like the magic book my first-grade teacher had used to teach me to read! We had studied a little about these in college, and I had used them during my student teaching, but I had spent most of my time learning about individualized reading programs and reading a lot of children's literature. I wondered if my college instructors knew I would find all of these materials in my first classroom. Tradition reigned in my thinking.

I spent afternoons looking through all the flashcards, workbooks, decoding worksheets, comprehension worksheets, study skill worksheets, and enrichment worksheets. Knowing it was important to show initiative and ability to

control and manage my class and programs, I "individualized" by making packets of ALL the worksheets. The presses rolled ... be-deep ... be-deep ...
be-deep. None of my second graders would miss a chance to learn. That manual
sure knew a lot.

Within weeks my students had learned the predictable system of doing
packets while I met with each of my six reading groups. When my reading program was under control, I started a Friday afternoon activity in which the children shared books and related home projects. They selected their own books,
read them in their free time or at home, and then told about them or read parts
to the class. They each received three positive comments about their presenta-
tions by calling on their peers after they shared. They loved this activity.

After a few months, I sensed that a disaster was about to happen. The children were getting so carried away with their excitement about our Friday afternoon sharing that the sessions kept getting longer. Sometimes they didn't have
enough time to complete their reading worksheets. In my panic that they might
get behind, I moved them along a little faster during reading time.

After several years, my spinal column was replaced by a sturdy metal spiral
binder, and I became a Super Basal, creating the best program for my children.
I discovered vocabulary and comprehension questions, which I used to produce my own worksheets to accompany the basal program. I even used other
publishers' basals and picked up on ideas my publisher had omitted. My children worked hard, and I was confident they would achieve the reward in return
for their hard work. They would, in the end, be lovers of reading. In the mean-
time, the students had assumed responsibility for running their Friday book
sharing sessions, which often provided me with time to correct worksheets and
workbooks. They really enjoyed this break from *reading*.

I had studied Bloom's Taxonomy in my masters program (Bloom 1956). I
learned how important it was for teachers to have a systematic procedure when
managing instruction and to know that children do not intuitively progress
from lower levels to higher levels without assistance. Learning about children's
sensory-psychomotor development, learning styles, and related reading problems helped me plan more appropriate ways for students to learn their letters,
sounds, and vocabulary through isolated sequencing and memory tasks. This
learning supported my classroom reading program, and I was able to add more
specific instruction to my program.

I studied Glasser (1969) and Adlerian psychology. My students spent much
class time in a big circle as they role-played problem-solving strategies, shared
the responsibility for whole-class rules and problems, and worked toward
responsible independence. I became increasingly sensitive to the self-esteem
need of my lower readers, continued to document deficits, applauded creative
writing efforts, and hugged them often, promising to help them read.

Then one day, TJ was working diligently at his worksheets but stopped to
tell me he liked the story he had overheard while eavesdropping on one of my
reading groups. TJ often daydreamed, and I felt I had to constantly keep him on
task. I was amazed that he could talk about a story that he had not been taught.
In a moment of weakness, I allowed him to get the book to show me what he
meant. He did and I panicked. I flipped my internal pages trying to find a
solution to the problem of having a child able to read and discuss a story prior

to doing worksheets. No information. My worries included wondering if he might also have read ahead in the individualized reading kit. I knew TJ had been having a tough time learning, and I sorted through every possible remedy in my Super Basal mind.

Then it hit me. *Who wasn't learning?*

I thought back to my university reading seminar where we had talked about individualized reading with trade books. We had learned how to organize and implement this program for a whole class. We had talked about the fact that there really was no need for ability groups, except maybe for skill work. We had discussed how the teacher could manage the program, make choices about which worksheets to use, and remain in control. I knew my students liked to read trade books. It made sense. I had learned to see so many of my students' deficits that I had often blinded myself from seeing their strengths and interests.

I took control and moved TJ to a higher group, made many worksheets optional for my students, and figured out a way to use just trade books. I felt a new sense of empowerment as a teacher. I felt I had begun to stand on my own two feet with my own backbone replacing the spiral basal backbone. I came to understand why the Friday afternoon book shares generated so much excitement. In fact, when the opportunity arose to take a position as a reading specialist, I jumped at the idea. I wanted to share my new learning with other teachers and help remedial students to value themselves as readers.

I took on the role of fixing children in closets. I celebrated their successes reading high-interest, low-vocabulary books that I had carefully prescribed. We created wonderful individual and small-group dictated stories for our reading enjoyment. I also provided plenty of time for isolated skill drills of discrete reading subskill weaknesses that I had determined from standardized testing. Meanwhile, I told other teachers what I had learned about being in control of reading instruction in the classroom. We went through the process of developing our own scope-and-sequence charts for teaching reading skills so we would not be so controlled by the basal reading series and could take control of our reading programs.

Then, when I enrolled in an advanced graduate degree program, I was introduced to Frank Smith's writing (1978). His work helped me to put myself in control of my own reading and my ability to value and evaluate my own thinking. I was beginning to see that my teaching was based too much on a deficit theory of learning. I became more comfortable with the idea of revision of thought without feeling I was inadequate and just correcting mistakes. I had a greater level of comfort taking risks and realizing I would continue to learn for the rest of my life.

I looked more closely at my teaching decisions about when to intervene with children's learning and when not to intervene. I became more conscious of myself as a decision maker and used many of my own resources when I decided to intervene in a child's reading development. After a decade of classroom and remedial teaching, I was observing my students and myself as readers and writers in many learning contexts. I was familiar with many instructional materials and tests on the market and was learning to evaluate their use. Professional reading and theoretical grounding helped me to develop the language to discuss the processes of reading and writing with students, parents, peers, and administrators. I relied on my learning experiences and used them to build bridges between my previously product-oriented thinking and my current process-oriented thinking. I felt confident looking at my curriculum guide or the old scope-and-sequence charts and deciding:

1. To teach a skill because the child was wrestling with it in a meaningful context,

2. To not teach a skill because the child was just beginning to play with that skill and showed no consistent need for intervention,

3. To teach a skill through an awareness session because the child was just beginning to play with the skill and might notice it if I put it into a meaningful context, or

4. To not teach a skill because the student was not showing any signs of playing with it or being ready for direct instruction to make sense.

My understanding of the process of reading continued to develop as I began to evaluate my teaching, testing, record keeping, and reporting to parents about what readers value. I was learning to articulate for myself and others the reasons an isolated skills approach to reading does not make sense, and that reading is a process that involves predicting, confirming, monitoring, revising, and integrating knowledge in endless contexts. This reading-process vocabulary was not even present in the traditional basal scope-and-sequence charts.

Rethinking Benjamin Bloom's hierarchy of skills, I realized that it was a very linear model. Inverting it made sense sometimes. At other times it just didn't make sense anymore. I noticed my students easily used higher levels of thinking when discussing books, a fact I had missed when working through the sequence of prepared basal reader questions. Students seemed to use different levels of thinking depending upon their needs and interests. Plus, they had opportunities to ask questions, and I had a chance to learn to listen.

I read books and articles by Ken and Yetta Goodman (1987), Nancie Atwell (1987), Donald Graves (1983), Judith Newman (1985), Gordon Wells (1985), and Ellen Blackburn (1984), who researched, developed, and validated new understandings and language in the field. They looked at the whole child as a learner. I developed a working knowledge of the whole-language philosophy and the processes of reading and writing. I learned the value of writing dialogue journal letters in response to reading, the importance of response to writing, and the relationships between reading and writing.

My Chapter 1 pull-out program environment changed to reflect my thinking. I developed small communities of learners who valued the process of reading and writing. I also tried to make my testing sessions more consistent with theory and research. When evaluating a child, I attempted to look at numerous literacy events in as many contexts as possible. I used a combination of student- and teacher-selected reading materials, along with materials from the content areas, when I was asked to evaluate a child in the older grades. Using an adapted miscue analysis for evaluating reading with pretellings, retellings, and discussion, I tried to focus on what the child could do. I analyzed spelling miscues by looking at developmental spelling stages rather than percent perfect. I recommended learning contexts and strategies (Cochrane et al. 1984) that might enhance the child's literacy development. I closely analyzed writing using a rubric that was similar to the analytic scoring guide used in Maine during the scoring of the fourth-grade state writing samples. I focused on building on what the child already knew by looking at writing in process, reading in process, and asking the child to reflect on learning.

I was finally learning! I became more cognizant of my decision-making processes and for the first time developed *my* philosophy of learning. I read, wrote, talked, and listened, trying to depend on my philosophical grounding to make my teaching decisions. Writing about my thinking and creating new formats to communicate student development was a new and intriguing learning experience. Through collaboration with colleagues involved in both classroom instruction and university instruction, I developed a report card (Figure 16–1) that was a piece of writing reflecting the culmination of my current thinking in 1987 (Bailey et al. 1988).

As I watched classroom teachers also changing to be increasingly in tune with current research, I struggled with the rationale of removing children from their meaningful and natural classroom learning contexts. In fact, I found I no longer believed in my own position as it was defined. There is a need for reading specialists to work as resources alongside teachers. However, I concluded the best situation for a reading specialist would be working with children in a classroom in which the teacher ascribed to current research and practice. There was no sense in trying to believe in remedial closet miracles.

The challenge of figuring out how to manage and explain classroom teaching/learning in a way that was consonant with current research drew me back to the classroom. After nine years as a reading specialist, I no longer felt comfortable pulling children from their classrooms. The need to be more consistent with my ever evolving philosophy guided my thinking, and I went back to classroom teaching in a school where the teachers shared a common philosophy and dedication to process-oriented learning. Teachers in my new building are in control of instruction. Student self-evaluation and goal setting are often at the core of instructional decisions. The classroom learning community is established so that everyone in it, including the teacher, is a member of the literacy club (Smith 1978).

My first task, as a classroom teacher, was to figure out how to keep all of my Chapter 1 and special education students in the classroom so they could continue to learn in the most natural and social context. I did not want them to have to go outside the classroom and think that their resources were in a special room. Rather, I wanted them to see the rich resources that are in the classroom and to believe that they themselves are rich resources; resource room children need to know they are resources. I invited the specialists to be a part of our classroom learning community, to work within the program already in progress (Hansen 1987). The children valued having more people in the classroom who could listen responsively to their reading and writing and to intervene in meaningful ways (Rhodes and Dudley-Marling 1988).

Figure 16–1

Supplementary reading program report card.

Observations About The Student As A Learner
Supplementary Reading Program Report
Reading Specialist: Janis Bailey

Student:_____   Year_____   Grade_____

	1	2	3	4
Seems to view self as an effective reader — during shared reading				
— during independent reading				
Seems to view self as an effective author — when dictating writing				
— during independent writing				
Takes Risks:				
As a reader in: –selecting books				
–predicting — using knowledge in own head (prior experience)				
— using text and/or pictures				
–figuring out unknowns:				
using meaning clues — in context				
— in own head (prior experience)				
using sentence structure clues (grammar, etc.)				
substituting a word with similar meaning				
using "sounding out"				
using word structure clues (endings; basewords, etc.)				
–revising thinking when "it doesn't make sense"				
–talking meaningfully about books — in retelling material read				
— in group discussion, sharing				
As a writer in: –choosing writing topics				
–producing meaningful writing				
–spelling with invented spelling to maintain meaning				
–revising writing to make it more meaningful				
–sharing own writing				
Chooses to pursue topics of interest				
Uses a variety of resources and literature to learn about self-selected topics				
Sticks with a plan — in reading				
— in writing				
Requests meaningful help — in reading				
— in writing				
Raises questions: — about books read or listened to by the student				
— about information others share in group				
— that may lead to new learning				

∠⁊ Effectively demonstrated by the student at this time.   ◢ Not a focus at this time.

Now that I am in a third-grade classroom I have many hard accountability questions to answer. It is a challenge, but I believe the resources I need to help me articulate the learning occurring in my classroom are within the classroom. There are no ability groupings, basal programs, or pull-out Chapter 1 and special education services. I'm determined to analyze the events in my classroom and to dream up new ways to better validate and communicate all of the things going on in our process-oriented environment. As a staff we are learning to evaluate our programs by developing student portfolios of literacy development and presenting our data in a more scientific, hard-data format to show constructively (Shannon 1989) that what we are doing makes sense and is good teaching and learning.

References

Atwell, Nancie. 1987. *In the Middle: Writing, Reading and Learning with Adolescents.* Portsmouth, NH: Boynton/Cook.

Bailey, Janis, et al. 1988. "Problem Solving Our Way to Alternative Evaluation Procedures." *Language Arts* 65(4): 364–373.

Blackburn, Ellen. 1984. "Common Ground: Developing Relationships between Reading and Writing." *Language Arts* 61(4):367–375.

Bloom, Benjamin. 1956. *Taxonomy of Educational Objectives; Cognitive Domain.* New York: Longmans Green and Co.

Cochrane, Orim, Donna Cochrane, Sharon Scalena, and Ethel Buchanan. 1984. *Reading, Writing and Caring.* New York: Richard C. Owen.

Glasser, William. 1969. *Schools Without Failure,* New York: Harper and Row.

Goodman, K., E. Smith, R. Meredith, and Y. Goodman. 1987. *Language and Thinking in School.* New York: Richard C. Owen.

Graves, Donald H. 1983. *Writing: Teachers and Children at Work.* Portsmouth, NH: Heinemann.

Hansen, Jane. 1987. *When Writers Read.* Portsmouth, NH: Heinemann.

Newman, Judith. 1985. *Whole Language: Theory in Use.* Portsmouth, NH: Heinemann.

Rhodes, Lynn K., and Curt Dudley-Marling. 1988. *Readers and Writers with a Difference: A Holistic Approach to Teaching Learning Disabled and Remedial Students.* Portsmouth, NH: Heinemann.

Shannon, Patrick. 1989. *Broken Promises: Reading Instruction in Twentieth-Century America.* Granby, MA: Bergin and Garvey.

Smith, Frank. 1978. *Reading without Nonsense.* New York: Teachers College Press.

Wells, Gordon. 1985. *The Meaning Makers: Children Learning Language.* Portsmouth, NH: Heinemann.

IV. Conversations

17. Redefining Our Role as Special Educators: Understandings Gained from Whole Language

Patricia Tefft Cousin
Linda Prentice
Ellen Aragon

Cathy Leonard
Lisa Ann Rose
Timothy Weekley

A group of special educators, new to whole-language instruction, sat in a small circle in a graduate language arts class. They brainstormed and then recorded areas of personal interest. This activity provided a way for them to define their questions and concerns about language instruction.

"How do you work with a variety of books with only one Big Book in the classroom?" asked Margaret, a teacher of primary-aged special needs students.

John, a high school resource teacher, said, "The regular class social studies teacher wants the students to memorize vocabulary for a test. How can I rationalize using whole language in the resource program when I am trying to help the students be successful in their regular class?"

Nancy, a teacher of upper elementary students added, "How do you keep everyone working and interested when you have a class with varied abilities?"

"I have the same problem," said Barbara, a teacher of students with severe behavior problems. "Also, how do I teach my students to sit and read a book when they hate reading? I have several students who refuse to read for more than a few minutes."

These comments and questions about holistic teaching are familiar to us. We asked many of the same questions ourselves when we were first introduced to the theories underlying whole-language instruction. When the six of us got together, we discussed how we applied these holistic understandings about language and learning in our own teaching of special-needs learners. As a result of our applications, we developed different views about learning and teaching. In changing our classrooms, we recognized the potential of whole language, for us as well as our students.

Linda put it rather succinctly: "Special-needs students are students who have suffered as a result of the system. They are perceived to be brain damaged to some small or large degree. Instead of looking at where the system has failed, we have traditionally implemented a medical model regarding these children—we believe the failure lies within the brain of the child. We are obtuse in our vision. We rarely look at how we work with students or where we can improve. Whole language allows, probably for the first time, a setting where these children can center upon their personal needs and interests. Through reading, writing, and responding to literature, students construct meaning from universal themes."

We don't offer a panacea to all of the problems confronting teachers of special-needs learners, but, rather, an invitation to join with us as we discuss our work with such students. We hope that, through the discussion that follows, you will gain some insight regarding:

1. Our prior educational and teaching experiences.
2. The factors we viewed as essential to our change.
3. What whole language offered us.
4. Where we are heading in the future.

Prior educational and teaching experiences

Traditionally, we have taught special-needs learners by focusing on their deficits. This notion evolved from theoretical views of teaching and learning based on the behavioral, medical, psychological, and learning-strategies models, all termed by Poplin as reductionist (1988a, 1988b). Teachers espousing this view break down ideas, concepts, and skills into parts. The goal of the curriculum is for students to master these defined sets of skills in each area of study. Special educators particularly emphasize identifying and remediating the specific skills that students have not mastered (Walmsley and Walp 1990).

In contrast, whole language is based on a view of learning as a transactional experience, rather than a transfer of information from teacher to student (Rosenblatt 1978). The teacher focuses first on supporting students in understanding the functions of language in their lives. They then learn about appropriate conventions as they engage in using oral and written language. Their classroom reading and writing involves the same types of reading and writing that we do outside of school (Altwerger, Edelsky, and Flores 1987). Students encountering difficulty with reading and writing need more support and additional time to accomplish the tasks rather than a remedial skills approach (Walmsley and Walp 1990). Whole-language teachers value each learner and the prior knowledge and background experiences each brings to the classroom. Because of this contrast in basic theoretical beliefs about how to support students encountering difficulty, whole language has been infrequently discussed in the special education literature.

We each had experiences organizing our classrooms and teaching based on a reductionist view of learning, and were frustrated by the results. We observed our students uninterested in learning, acting inappropriately, and making little progress. While students learned the skills, many were unable to synthesize and use them in an integrated manner to actually read and write. Several of us were bored with our own classrooms.

"The system of skills teaching, with objectives and carefully measured increments of change, was easy to follow. It was a safe cage, with boundaries and carefully plotted lines. I was fairly content with having my responsibilities as a teacher delineated," said Cathy.

"I taught and demonstrated preplanned lessons from the basal reader and the writing manual," added Tim.

"I began as a secondary history and political science teacher," commented Ellen. "My focus was on content-area reading, the understanding of sophisticated concepts and vocabulary, and how those concepts were related. I knew little about content-area strategies. I hated using a text that seemed to pull concepts apart. The students were expected to combine ideas and decide on their importance, too. It just didn't work."

However, to consider changes in our teaching was not easy. Some of us were firmly entrenched in the practices of skill-based teaching. Schon (1986) wrote, "When someone learns a practice, he is initiated into the traditions of a community of practitioners and the practice world they inhabit" (37). As special education teachers, we absorbed the common practices of teaching students with learning difficulties. As we changed our focus, we had to learn about and become involved in a new community of practice.

Factors viewed as essential to change

In various ways, we each became acquainted with the theories underlying whole language and the resulting implications for our classrooms. Graduate classes and staff development workshops were critical for each of us as part of our growing awareness of whole language. We were presented with new ways of looking at our students. We learned to refocus and look at what the students *could do,* rather than what they could not do.

From those initial exposures, we each explored a variety of avenues to learn more about whole language. We increased our professional reading, attended conferences and inservices, collaborated with other interested teachers, worked with curriculum specialists, and observed other teachers. Each of us learned in a unique context, but we all needed support from outside our classrooms. Just as we had learned about traditional views, we learned about new ideas by becoming immersed in a community of others exploring those ideas.

Ellen sums up the factors that supported her as a resource teacher using whole language as she co-taught with the regular classroom teacher: "Recent university classes were the most influential in changing my views. I believe special education reflects the status quo; we continue to use the same practices without much reflection. People have to be reeducated in order to change their beliefs. Secondly, professional literature, such as *In the Middle* (Atwell 1987), had a big influence on my ideas of teaching reading and writing. Finally, the regular education teachers and their willingness to work with us and our students proved to be a very powerful source of success, learning, and motivation."

As a result of gaining new information and applying it in our classes, we changed our views of teaching and learning or came back to a way of teaching that made sense to each of us.

Linda felt her preservice program did not emphasize theory. "Theoretical beliefs were undefined in my early years of teaching. I simply followed the directives in the teachers' editions. I did not have a true understanding until postgraduate work."

For Lisa and Pat, exposure to whole language was rather like a homecoming. Lisa said, "This approach was my natural way of teaching, but it had been squelched by my teacher education classes. As I gained confidence in my ability to work with children, I saw that I was effective when I became a facilitator of learning instead of a director. I learned to aid students in finding their own pathways of learning and development."

Pat had a similar experience. "When I began teaching kindergarten, the child was at the center of my teaching. But I changed to a skills-based model when I transferred to a special education class. I didn't trust my own beliefs and knowledge. I believed that these students needed a different approach. As time passed, I realized that a holistic approach would better serve these children. Whole language provided a resolution to the conflict I was experiencing in what I knew about learning and what I was doing in my classroom."

What whole language offered us

One main theme that emerged from our conversation was our belief that teachers change their classrooms when they observe that new perspectives and ideas make a difference with the children they teach. Observing changes in our students as we changed our classrooms was *the* critical factor that spurred us to continue our studies and learn about language. We changed our classrooms by incorporating holistic strategies and using alternative structures in our reading and writing programs. When we tried out strategies such as Written Conversation, Say Something, or Message Board, and when we implemented alternative structures such as Sustained Reading Time and Writer's Workshop, our students actually engaged in reading and writing (Atwell 1987; Gilles et al. 1987; Harste, Short, and Burke 1989). The strategies provided opportunities for us to support our students' strengths rather than deficits. We want to share some of those changes through stories about our classrooms.

Changes in students.　Tim discussed the growth he's observed in his students: "I have observed an increase in verbalization. My students now predict outcomes about stories. They enjoy reading. Books are now an important part of our classroom. They have also become authors. Let me give you an example. When we first started using journals, Brian and Steven, both students with severe language and cognitive difficulties, copied words they saw displayed in the room. After a time they began to 'scribble-write' and then tell us what they had written. Now we can actually read their invented spelling as they write. No one ever believed they could make this much progress. No one assumed that they could be writers."

Lisa joined in the conversation. "My students now enjoy literature and writing. They have become increasingly sophisticated in their predictions and critical and interpretive thinking abilities. Whole language has given them back their confidence and power as students and learners. They are no longer afraid to voice their opinions. They are constantly surprising themselves with their own capabilities and levels of understanding."

"Lauren is a good example of what has happened in my classroom for students with emotional problems," continued Lisa. "When Lauren first came into my class, she rarely spoke. She had been abused for a number of years. After several weeks of writing only one or two sentences in her journal, she began to use it as a catharsis. She began to place her journal on my desk, knowing I would respond. Lauren was unable to communicate orally, but found a voice through her writing. We became very close over the next six months as she shared her pain. Eventually, she was able to address me verbally. She now discusses her problems in our group sessions, and her journal is filled with the normal trials and tribulations of adolescence. Her journal was not the only reason for this change, but it did contribute greatly to her healing process."

Ellen talked about her students: "Whole language has been the key to our successful integration of resource students into the regular classroom. In the first year of the collaborative program, we saw their standardized test scores increase in every area. These increases were more significant in the language arts areas. More importantly, we saw special education students who no longer felt they were 'speds.' Confidence soared, self-esteem increased, and they enjoyed a rich curriculum. They studied literature and participated in group experiences, which increased their reading and writing skills. Their behavior improved as they moved back into the regular classroom."

"Let me tell you about James," said Ellen. "He's a seventh grader who encounters great difficulty in spelling. In the past he never wrote anything more than a sentence. His instructional objectives were focused on remediating his spelling problem. Now, as a part of the regular language arts class, he is a participant in writer's workshop. He leads the entire class in our discussions about pieces of literature we've read. The ideas and concepts presented in his written responses are among the most sophisticated in the class. While James still has difficulty with spelling, this is being taken care of as a natural part of the editing process. James is now able to capitalize on his strengths in interpretation."

Changes in our teaching. Likewise, changes occurred for us as teachers. Just as whole language offers new potentials for students, it offers new potentials for teachers as well.

Cathy said, "The biggest contribution of whole-language theory and practice is that it has given me the freedom to offer choices and not be afraid I'll miss a specific skill in sequence. The whole-language emphasis gives me the opportunity to examine my curriculum and do things with the class that excite all of us."

"About two months ago," she told us, "I apologized to my students for overemphasizing memorization of terms and underemphasizing the broad concepts we covered during our unit of study on rocks. I told them that when I had gone home, I had tried to think of a good reason why they needed to memorize these definitions and I couldn't think of any. I told them I wanted them to understand how to go to the library and find information any time they needed it. The upshot is that I find I am continually asking the questions What do they need this for? Is it information they will parrot and soon forget or a concept they will be able to grasp and use?"

Linda added, "I have become a better teacher. I am no longer as rigid as I once was. I listen more to my students and try to incorporate their interests into the curriculum. I give my students responsibility for their learning. My teaching has changed in that, through my studies and a continual refinement of my philosophy, I have elevated the learner to the center and stepped back as an authority figure so that children have more control over their own learning. I like to believe that I am more a facilitator and guide than teacher. While there are still many restrictions in the teaching profession, there are a variety of ways teachers can allow students more choices throughout the day."

Linda told us what this meant in her classroom: "Although I am required to cover the literature anthology, I use cooperative groups and each group chooses the stories it will cover. Students also decide how they will share their responses with the rest of the class. They are not only choosing stories that match their interests but also learning about social relationships as they negotiate what they will read. And, in writer's workshop, each student chooses a topic to write about."

We believe that this way of approaching teaching is much less stressful since we no longer have to know all of the answers. *Teaching has become a process rather than a routine.* A natural part of that process is accepting and building on what is most important in our classrooms during a particular period of time. We make those decisions as the individuals who best know our students.

Looking to the future

The contexts in which each of us works is varied, yet we all recognized the need to guide our own change. We each took different risks based on our own individual direction. As we finished our conversation, we talked about what we might suggest to others.

Ellen said, "Change methods one at a time. Become a risk taker and allow students to inform the decision-making process."

"Advice I would include would be to go slowly, adapt little by little," added Cathy. "I would emphasize the idea that it's good to be a teacher who continues to learn."

Tim's suggestions focused on changes in the classroom: "Have high expectations of students, surround them with print and books, accept students' best attempts, and provide opportunities for students to interact meaningfully with texts and each other."

Change is always very complex because a multitude of factors influences and affects each situation. All of us had to make individual decisions about what to implement in our classroom. We are not satisfied, but, rather, we are constantly developing new ideas and asking new questions as we continue to learn.

"I'm at another questioning point," said Cathy.

"I want to create a supportive learning environment, give up control, and allow students to experiment with writing," commented Tim.

Lisa added, "Whole language to me doesn't mean you have a whole-language lesson plan you develop and use year after year. Rather, whole language means that I need to keep in touch with the most relevant, updated material and books and incorporate them any way I can to keep high-level interest."

"I have a lot to experience and learn. I feel many changes are going to occur in my focus, but my basic beliefs about learning and teaching are intact," summed up Ellen.

Redefinitions

As we discussed the contexts in which each of us learned, we recognized that we are not very different from the students we teach—we need support, time, others to work with on areas of concern, a willingness to take risks, and an interest in learning. Schon (1986) proposed that uncertainty and uniqueness characterize the actual practice of a profession. He argues that these are central to the artistry that really makes up what we do. This concept makes a great deal of sense to us as we talk about the students we see in our classrooms. There are no simple explanations about why they are having reading and writing difficulties; likewise, there are no simple solutions. Our involvement in whole language has provided new ways for us to support these students, and, in the process, redefined our role as special educators.

References

Altwerger, B., C. Edelsky, and B. Flores. 1987. "Whole Language, What's New." *Reading Teacher* 41: 144–154.

Atwell, N. 1987. *In the Middle: Writing, Reading and Learning with Adolescents.* Portsmouth, NH: Boynton/Cook.

Harste, J., K. Short, and C. Burke. 1989. *Creating Classrooms for Authors.* Portsmouth, NH: Heinemann.

Gilles, C., et al. 1987. *Whole Language Strategies for Secondary Students.* New York: Richard C. Owens.

Poplin, M. 1988a. "The Reductionist Fallacy in Learning Disabilities: Replicating the Past by Reducing the Present." *Journal of Learning Disabilities* 21: 385–448.

Poplin, M. 1988b. "Holistic/Constructivist Principles of the Teaching/Learning Process: Implications for the Field of Learning Disabilities." *Journal of Learning Disabilities* 21: 401–416.

Rosenblatt, L. 1978. *The Reader, the Text, and the Poem.* Carbondale, IL: Southern Illinois University Press.

Schon, D. 1986. *Educating the Reflective Practitioner.* San Francisco: Jossey-Bass.

Walmsley, S., and T. Walp. 1990. "Integrating Literature and Composing into the Language Arts Curriculum: Philosophy and Practice." *Elementary School Journal* 90: 251–274.

18. Have Dignity for Yourself

Carmelita Chee
Clark Etsitty
Daisy Kiyaani

Lee Kiyaani
Louise Lockard
Laura Tsosie

"What does it mean to be literate in Piñon, Navajo Nation, Arizona? How can we prepare our students and our own children to become literate adults?" These are important questions because they allow us to re-search our literate histories. Our questions allow us to use what we have learned about the past to teach the children of the Piñon community. By sharing "dangerous memories" (McLaren 1988), hopes, dreams, and prayers, the discussion becomes a liberation education (Shor 1990) for those involved.

On June 1, 1988, five teachers and a social worker met to share stories of the literacy that shaped our lives and led us to become teachers. We have worked at Piñon Elementary School since it opened in the fall of 1984. Clark Etsitty, school social worker, began efforts to construct the school in 1978. Laura Tsosie and Carmelita Chee are special education teachers in the intermediate grades. They attended Piñon BIA School as children and were teachers at the BIA School before Piñon Public School was built. Lee Kiyaani, eighth-grade social studies teacher, and his wife Daisy Kiyaani, fifth-grade teacher, taught at Rough Rock Demonstration School before Piñon Public School opened. Louise Lockard, second-grade teacher, transcribed and edited the text of the discussion.

Louise: What does it mean to be literate here in Piñon? How can we prepare our students and our own children to become literate, functioning adults?

Clark: I have something that might be entirely outside the question. But we were talking about it this morning. We were saying that there are some principles that we have in mind as far as school is concerned. There are four notable principles; ways to go about life. The key words are in Navajo. The first one is: *iliigo a'daanitsinikees doo 'adahodinilzin do.* Have dignity for yourself. You are precious. Your life is sacred and holy. The holy ones have created you, and you have a rightful place. You are a part of your parents and grandparents and clan relatives. The second one is: *niho ni yoo do.* Be ethical, moral, and prudent. Do what is right and lawful and legal. Recall wise teachings and sayings of your people in the society you live in. Have a purpose in what you do in your life. The third one is: *Nitsi'nikas do.* Use your intelligence and knowledge. Be rational and analytical. You are unique because you have a mind to analyze. The fourth one is: *Nihi ni' yoo do.* Develop and maintain your physical and mental strength. These are the sayings that our people have said back before the days of formal schooling. As we were talking about it this morning these could be revised, expanded upon, interpreted in terms of our present life.

Along with this, since you were talking about parents and how they affect their children's learning here at school, I have a personal thought. This goes back to some historical events we as Navajos have undergone. Being convinced, believing, this is very important. For our children to succeed in school, their parents have an overwhelming responsibility. This is a most important time in their lives and important time for their children's lives. Their support is so much needed in the schools. This is comparable with the infamous disease that prevailed in the 1920s: tuberculosis. There was a big campaign to eradicate the disease. One of our leaders, Mrs. Annie Wauneka, went out and educated the Navajo people. She went out and taught in the way Navajos could understand. They were so convinced by her teaching, that this disease was eradicated. They have to be so convinced that education is very important.

Lee: How do parents help their children read and write? I have come to get the idea that we need to educate the parents about the importance of education for themselves and for their children. Once they get involved, they'll have their own interpretation and understanding of what education is all about. The child will get a great amount of support, not no support at all. The child needs that kind of support. At present, students get this kind of support just at school. The teacher tells them, "You can do it, yes you can." When they get home they're really not getting that kind of support. The parents say, "When you come home, your traditional education takes over." I don't know what traditional means to these particular parents; hauling wood, bringing in the water, taking the sheep out. These are the chores the kids can do. They just leave it to the kids. The kids are on their own. They just kind of interpret, feel their own way. They are avoided some way. They're not getting any support. When they try to do the school work, ask questions about science or math, they are avoided some way. The parent says, "That kind of work you should have done at school." The child is smart enough to know what kind of game he's going to play with them. The kids start playing around, go after the sheep, simply get away from home, go to their grandparents'. Discipline-wise, the child is not getting the full support. The parental support is being downgraded by the school. All around, the child is not getting the kind of support he or she should be given. It's like a one-half effort.

Daisy: We keep referring back to the statement, "We're not getting support at home." As a Reservation, we are removed from the mainstream. We go back to what we went through as a people. History tells us a lot of things have happened to us. At one time we were a strong people. In a lot of ways we've made changes as a people. We still have our language. We still have our beliefs. We still have our ways of living. Reservation status put us at a disadvantage. It removed us from everything else. Although our people have agreed to receive education, it seems the type of education has been limited. It really doesn't prepare youngsters to live out in the mainstream. The focus of education in the 1950s and 1960s was preparing kids for menial jobs. Through the treaty our people agreed to education. But schools were limited and inferior in the sense that our own ways were never included in the educational programs. Now we're trying to go back and look at the whole thing and find out where we feel things may have gone wrong. We're trying to design education so our kids will be more successful learners than in the past. We're trying to reidentify with the four areas Clark pointed out. When education was introduced to us, values got lost in the shuffle. Kids need to know values plus our own past. This would give them some understanding. They would have something to work for rather than just be here every day not really having anything to look towards. To help our kids be successful, they should just use their own environment right here—science concepts, geography, and history—then other things will make a lot more sense.

Carmelita: I agree with you, Daisy. Our history has a lot to do with the way things are now. During your time, the three of you [Daisy, Clark, Lee] went to school off the Reservation. Your parents never had a say in how you were educated. It was only very recently that public schools started coming onto the Reservation. That's when the parents started realizing they should have some kind of input into their children's education. They don't really know how to get themselves involved. It seems like in the past people said, "Yes, the government has promised to educate us." I don't think when the kids were at school they were taught these principles. Now when they're at an age when they're parents themselves, they don't really know what to teach their children.

Clark: Someone here on this panel mentioned that, at the onset of education, school was really foreign to our people. In the first days, the policemen were out there on horseback taking children to school. The parents resisted this. There was adversity. There might still be some differences. Formal education was considered to be opposed to traditional education. As far as that is concerned, it is our responsibility to instill the value of formal education to the point where we ought to have more reverence. Reverence not only in talk, but reverence in coming to school, reverence staying in school. Navajos depend on ceremonies, prayers. It's going to have to take that kind of reverence to make a whole lot of difference.

Louise: We agree that the history of school hasn't been a happy one for Navajo children. Daisy, you were taken away from home at an early age.

You lived away from home for many years. What encouragement can you give your own children? How can you sweeten up school for them?

Daisy: I, for one, I had to strive for what I wanted. I wanted an education so much. That was just a driving force for me. That value influences my own kids. When they were young I was going through college. I was a model to them. That's the way you counsel them, too. In my husband's family they say, "Do good. Do well. Strive for the best." They see it in the family. I tell my kids about some of the more unpleasant things I experienced. I had to sacrifice. I had to leave home when I was nine years old. I didn't know a word of English. I was taken away to Oklahoma nine months out of the year. You got to the point when you kind of looked down on what you were. It's a good example of being brainwashed. I was able to save myself. I didn't fall into that.

Lee: We continue to teach the values of the people in our own particular area where we're from. We try to make the children feel proud of their origins, of their roots. If the child is being supported and encouraged, and they have communications established with their parents, they will be able to do a lot of things. If the parents have that contact, their children will achieve a lot of things. The treaty of 1868 said that the soldiers had to hunt down the little Navajos and take them to the boarding school. I've heard stories about putting the children in a wagon, handcuffing them, and transporting them to Ft. Apache.

We talked about the Five Year Program in the 1950s, an off-Reservation vocational training program for laundry workers, shoe repairmen, maids, and potato pickers. In the 1960s, more emphasis was placed on high school. People keep telling us, "You need better skills because of technology." There is great emphasis now on post-secondary schools. The parent now pushing the little one says, "I want to see you in college." They want the pride of sending their child through college. With that they're encouraging their kids. The new generation of parents, they're on that track. I don't know what the next century will bring. We're beginning to awaken to the world around us. We will progress. We want scientists, doctors, lawyers. We're involved in this thing. It is coming around.

Carmelita: You wonder what parents do to make their kids want to go to college and be self-sufficient.

Louise: What do you do with your own children?

Laura: I've done a lot of reading with them ever since they were young. I talk with them about anything they want to know about. If I don't know, I say, "Maybe we can find what you're trying to get answered." I am a model to my kids. I always sit down and read. They watch me. They pick up ideas. They have this attitude; they can read and write. They really have developed. They can pick up any book and read it. Even though my parents were uneducated, they have encouraged me to learn a language

I wasn't familiar with. I put in all the effort to learn it. When I was in fourth grade, a letter was written to them. They said, "Here's a letter. Can you read it to us?" I read the letter the best I could and interpreted it to them. At the end they said, "From now on, keep on trying. We know you'll do it."

Even though I went through a lot, I still push myself to learn more. In a way, I'm not that literate, but I can do anything that's relevant to me. I'm sure these kids are going through the same thing. We try to push onto them things they're not familiar with. If we try to provide something relevant to them at school and at home I'm sure these kids will become literate kids—literate in Navajo and even in the dominant society.

Clark: As far as success is concerned, is it being literate? I've seen family set-ups where kids were productive whether the parents were formally educated or not. Whenever I see some good, positive factors I try to assess them. In those homes, the unique thing about the families is they are traditionally sound. The mothers and fathers are pretty well established. They have a savvy and a belief unique to them. Somebody within the family structure knows something. Prayer is universal. People can't do without it.

Lee: They have to have strong roots to fall back on.

Clark: In my years of college, I went down to Arizona State University. For three years I did quite well. As far as limited English, I was a prime example. When it got to where the lessons were in-depth and intense, I just couldn't hack it. I broke off from school to work in Rough Rock. There I was totally immersed in language and people. There was a lot of work done with resource people. There was no holding back on language. I helped in the translation of some stories. In two years, there was an improvement in how I spoke Navajo; my whole thought process changed. I thought for the better. I think my Navajo language has a place.

Six years have passed since we came to Piñon from Chinle, Rough Rock, Phoenix, and Piñon Boarding School. Many of our memories of schooling are dangerous memories, set aside because we have recess duty or because we need popcorn for a basketball tournament. The conversation recorded here is a beginning. Like teachers everywhere, we need to make more time to talk with each other about our hopes and dreams.

This year we worked across grade levels to teach thematic science units in Navajo and English. We invited parents to teach the students about native plants. Lee and Daisy Kiyaani taught a social studies unit about The Long Walk, an event in Navajo history that has influenced present social conditions on the Reservation. Laura Tsosie and Carmelita Chee worked with a cluster of special education students in fourth-, fifth-, and sixth-grade classrooms. Their students published books of stories they had learned from their grandmothers. Clark Etsitty invited Judge Bluehouse to talk with groups of students about substance abuse. The judge asked the students, "What are your plans for the future?"

Daisy Kiyaani said, "Our education was limited and inferior in the sense that our ways were never included in the educational programs. We're trying to go back and look at the whole thing and find out where we feel things may have gone wrong. We're trying to design education so our kids will be more successful learners." As teachers, we wish to raise our collective voices and share the literacy that has shaped our lives and led us to become teachers. Laura Tsosie's father encouraged her when, as a fourth grader, she read and translated a letter for him. He continues to support her now that she has become a teacher. He says, "I always hoped there would be teachers like you." We find support and encouragement in sharing our stories. We can extend this support to include our students in the community of learners at Piñon. We can find our dignity in our own experience.

References

Heath, S. B. 1988. "Being Literate in America: A Sociohistorical Perspective." In *Issues of Literacy: A Research Perspective,* Thirty-fourth Yearbook of the National Reading Conference, Rochester, NY.

McLaren, Peter. 1988. "The Liminal Servant and the Ritual Roots of Critical Pedagogy." *Language Arts* 65: 164–179.

Philips, S. U. 1983. *The Invisible Culture: Communication in Classroom and Community on the Warm Springs Indian Reservation.* New York: Longman.

Scollon, R., and S. B. K. Scollon. 1981. *Narrative, Literacy and Face in Inter-Ethnic Communication.* Norwood, NJ: Ablex.

Shor, Ira. 1990. "Liberation Education: An Interview with Ira Shor." *Language Arts* 67: 342–352.

Taylor, D., and C. Dorsey-Gaines. 1988. *Growing Up Literate.* Portsmouth, NH: Heinemann.

List of Contributors

Ellen Aragon teaches resource and regular education students at Cucumonga Junior High, Rancho Cucumonga, California.

Janis Ivanowsky Bailey, a former reading specialist, teaches third grade at Stratham Memorial School, Stratham, New Hampshire.

Carmelita Chee is an intermediate special education teacher at Piñon Elementary School, Piñon, Navajo Nation, Arizona.

Patricia Tefft Cousin teaches graduate courses in special education and reading at California State University, San Bernardino, California.

Marie Dionisio teaches sixth-grade remedial reading students at Louis M. Klein Middle School, Harrison, New York.

Clark Etsitty is the school social worker at the Piñon Elementary School, Piñon, Navajo Nation, Arizona.

Esther Sokolov Fine, formerly a special educator, is a primary teacher at Downtown Alternative School, Toronto, Ontario, Canada.

Alfreda B. Furnas is a resource room teacher at Eustis Elementary School, Eustis, Florida.

Kenneth S. Goodman is a professor of education in the Program for Language and Literacy at the University of Arizona, Tucson, Arizona.

Donald H. Graves is a professor of education at the University of New Hampshire, Durham, New Hampshire.

Linda Hoyt is a curriculum specialist for the Beaverton Schools, Beaverton, Oregon.

Ilene Seeman Johnson teaches seventh- and eighth-grade special education students at Louis M. Klein Middle School, Harrison, New York.

Daisy Kiyaani teaches fifth grade at Piñon Elementary School, Piñon, Navajo Nation, Arizona.

Lee Kiyaani teaches eighth-grade social studies at Piñon Elementary School, Piñon, Navajo Nation, Arizona.

Louise Lockard, formerly a second-grade teacher, now teaches seventh- and eighth-grade English at Piñon Elementary School, Piñon, Navajo Nation, Arizona.

Cathy Leonard teaches students identified as learning handicapped at Cypress Elementary School, Fontana, California.

Linda Prentice teaches language arts at Golden Valley Middle School, San Bernardino, California.

Michael Quinn, formerly a learning disabilities specialist, is now the assistant director of special education in Pembroke, New Hampshire.

Karen Robinson, formerly a Chapter 1 teacher and principal, is now a fourth-grade teacher at Woodstock School, Bryant Pond, Maine.

Tom Romano, formerly a high school English teacher, is a doctoral candidate at the University of New Hampshire, Durham, New Hampshire.

Lisa Ann Rose teaches students identified as emotionally handicapped at Serrano Middle School, San Bernardino, California.

Susan Stires, formerly a resource room teacher and language arts consultant, is a primary teacher at The Center for Teaching and Leaning, Edgecomb, Maine.

Bonnie S. Sunstein, a doctoral candidate at the University of New Hampshire, Durham, New Hampshire, also teaches undergraduate English at Rivier College, Nashua, New Hampshire.

M. Joan Throne is an intermediate teacher in the Fairfax County Public Schools, Fairfax, Virginia.

Laura Tsosie is an intermediate special education teacher at Piñon Elementary School, Piñon, Navajo Nation, Arizona.

William L. Wansart is a professor of special education at the University of New Hampshire, Durham, New Hampshire.

Timothy Weekley teaches students identified as severely handicapped at Hillside Elementary School, San Bernardino, California.